ISOTOPES IN BIOLOGY

ISOTOPES IN BIOLOGY

by GEORGE WOLF

Department of Nutrition and Food Science
Massachusetts Institute of Technology
Cambridge, Massachusetts

ACADEMIC PRESS · NEW YORK and LONDON

ACADEMIC PRESS, INC.
111 Fifth Avenue, New York, New York 10003

United Kingdom Edition published by
ACADEMIC PRESS, INC. (LONDON) LTD.
Berkeley Square House, London W1X 6BA

LIBRARY OF CONGRESS CATALOG CARD NUMBER: 64-24668

Fourth Printing, 1969

PRINTED IN THE UNITED STATES OF AMERICA

PREFACE

The rapid rate of progress during the last decade in biology, especially at the molecular level, has provided new and more fundamental insights into living systems. Many of the important discoveries which have redefined and broadened our concepts of biological phenomena have been inextricably related to the development of new experimental techniques and instrumentation. Not the least among these has been the wide application of isotopes as labels or analytical tools in biological research.

Isotopes have been extensively used as tracers in the investigation of biological phenomena, ranging from the gross to the molecular. Numerous textbooks (several of which are listed at the end of the first chapter) have been published on this subject alone. There is clearly a need for a simple elementary account of the use of isotopes in biology, primarily as an introduction to this important area.

The present volume is intended to fulfill this need not only for the beginning student in biology but also for the many graduate students and scientists who may be entering this field of research. This work has been designed to serve as a supplementary source of information rather than as a definitive textbook.

The particularly wide and fruitful application of isotopes in biochemistry and other aspects of molecular biology, as well as the author's own major research interests in intermediary metabolism, have been sufficient reason for the emphasis on these subjects here. The broad subject of *radiation biology,* which deals with the effects of radiation on living matter, has been intentionally omitted. Finally, it should be noted that the details of instrumentation, preparation of samples, and assay methods have not been described. They are intended to be the subject of another book in this series.

* * *

The author, Dr. George Wolf, is by training and experience ideally suited for this presentation of isotopes in biology. He was for eleven years a staff member through the rank of associate professor in the Radiocarbon Laboratory of the University of Illinois. These were the early years of isotope methodology when many of the standard methods used today were being worked out. At Illinois he taught a lecture and laboratory course on the use of isotopes in biology, biochemistry, and nutrition, and acted as consultant to students and staff in the use of isotopes in their research. He is now associate professor of Physiological Chemistry at the Massachusetts Institute of Technology, where he teaches a graduate course in isotope methodology. His research work has been in biochemistry, particularly the area of intermediary metabolism, studied with the use of isotopes.

ALVIN NASON, EDITOR

CONTENTS

Introduction

Scientific discoveries are neither good nor bad. It is the use that is made of them that determines our moral judgment. Atomic fission was discovered in the 1930's. In the unfolding of the mushroom cloud over Hiroshima, in the rain of death, and the fear it has brought to the world since, we have the most glaring example ever of the misuse of a discovery. However, there followed many other consequences, for instance, the making of radioactive isotopes. From the time these became available, experimental biology, and especially biochemistry, has made meteoric progress, contributing a whole new branch of biology—molecular biology—on the way.

1. WHAT ARE ISOTOPIC TRACERS AND WHY USE THEM?

What are isotopic tracers? Let us begin by saying that they are a species of matter exactly identical in all respects to normal matter, excepting in one property: isotopic tracer atoms have a tag or label on them which makes them instantly recognizable amongst a large number of normal atoms. This label is either radioactivity (radioactive isotopes), or a different atomic weight (stable isotopes). Thus the isotopic atoms become tags which, when added to normal atoms, can make them detectable, and thereby reveal the course they follow in chemical or biochemical reactions. In other words, one can then *trace* the behavior of these atoms, the isotope being the *tracer*.

A distinction must be made between the use of isotopes as tracers, and the effect of the isotopes, especially their radioactivity, on the system under investigation. This book is concerned only with isotopes as tracers and not with their effect. In fact, it is one of the conditions of their use that they will behave exactly like normal atoms, and not exert an effect *as isotopes*. A large amount of work has been done on the subject of the effect of radiation on living and nonliving matter, a subject termed radiation biology and radiation chemistry. However, we are here concerned only with the use of isotopes as labels and analytical tools.

Why use isotopes? It should always be borne in mind that they are only tools in biological research, and not the end of the research itself. The question to be asked should be: what is the biological problem and can an isotope help in its solution? The question should not be: how can we adapt our biological problem so that an isotope can be used?

Isotopes as tools in biological research have been aptly compared to the microscope (Broda, 1960). Such a comparison can serve to keep a sense of proportion in an evaluation of isotopic methods. On the one hand, the development of the microscope in the seventeenth century has led to an enormous surge forward in biology through the discovery of cells and microorganisms. On the other hand, no biologist would regard microscopy as a panacea for all problems, or develop it into a science for its own sake.

And yet why are isotopes so much more powerful than other existing methods, such as microscopy or spectrophotometry? The reason lies in the truly fantastic sensitivity with which they can be detected, and the fact that observations made with them lend themselves readily to quantitative measurement.

As an example, take a millimole of commercially available and inexpensive glucose labeled with radioactive carbon, with radioactivity of 1 millicurie (units explained in Chapter II). This amount (180 mg.) would fill about the tip of a spatula. It could be evenly mixed with 2000 lb. of ordinary (nonradioactive) glucose, a dilution of 5 million times. On making a radioactivity assay on about 10 mg. of this mixture (a minute sample, suitable for radioactivity determination with a Geiger-Mueller counter), one would still find appreciable radioactivity, giving about 500 counts per minute.

As another example, one might consider the much more energetic radioactive cobalt (cobalt-60). Comar (1955) describes an experiment in which the distribution of 0.1 mg. of this element in isotopic form in a 1000-lb. cow was easily mapped. Normally a cow eats about 1 mg. of this element per day, and one could imagine the insuperable difficulties in having to devise *chemical* methods for the analysis in a cow of such amounts of cobalt.

2. HISTORICAL

The beginnings of tracer methods on a very limited scale date back to the early 1920's, when Hevesy and his co-workers used naturally occurring isotopes (lead, bismuth, and thorium) and studied their distribution and metabolism in plants and animals. It is remarkable that most of tracer methodology in use at present was devised by these pioneers of forty years ago. When artificial radioactivity was discovered by Joliot and Curie in the early 1930's, Hevesy was again the first to study the distribution of radioactively labeled phosphate in animals. This experiment marks the true beginning of the use of isotopes as intended in the present discussion. A compound, sodium phosphate, which occurs naturally in the animal body, was traced in its movements and reactions in the body, by administration of a minutely small dose of labeled sodium phosphate.

At about the same time, Hevesy also used deuterium, a nonradioactive (stable) isotope of hydrogen, incorporated into water, and studied its distribution and elimination. Schoenheimer greatly expanded the use of deuterium and, as Hevesy had done for the radioactive isotopes, laid the foundation for the methodology of the stable isotopes. Schoenheimer's investigations with heavy nitrogen led to the concept of *the dynamic state of body constituents* (see Chap. VI, Sect. III-1), an idea that revolutionized biochemistry.

Carbon is the element of which, fundamentally, all living matter is made. The first to use a carbon isotope (C^{11}, half-life 20.5 min.) in a biological experiment were Ruben, Hassid, and Kamen in 1939. The isotope was made in a cyclotron, and the study was the uptake of labeled carbon dioxide by algae in the process of photosynthesis. The long-lived isotope of carbon, C^{14}, also was first detected and made by Ruben and Kamen in 1940. Later processes (to be described in Chapter I) for the manufacture of C^{14} by the atomic reactor derive from the pioneering discoveries of these investigators.

Today, the enormous flow of neutrons from atomic reactors in many countries provides the biological researcher with an abundance of isotopic elements and compounds. Firms making labeled compounds to satisfy the needs, and often the passing whims and fancies, of experimental biologists are flourishing, as are the many industries that supply the instruments and equipment for handling and assaying isotopes. Radioactivity counters and scalers have become standard equipment of all biological laboratories.

REFERENCES

Broda, E. (1960). "Radioactive Isotopes in Biochemistry," p. 1. Am. Elsevier, New York.

Comar, C. L. (1955). "Radioisotopes in Biology and Agriculture," p. 4. McGraw-Hill, New York.

GENERAL REFERENCES

(More advanced texts)

Readers interested in advanced reading on the subject of this book may find the following books helpful:

Aronoff, S. (1956). "Techniques in Radiobiochemistry." Iowa State College Press, Ames, Iowa.

Broda, E. (1960). "Radioactive Isotopes in Biochemistry." Am. Elsevier, New York.

Calvin, M. (1949). "Isotopic Carbon." Wiley, New York.

Catch, J. R. (1961). "Carbon-14 Compounds." Butterworths, London.

Chase, G. D. (1959). "Principles of Radioisotope Methodology." Burgess, Minneapolis, Minnesota.

Ciba Foundation (1951) Conference on "Isotopes in Biochemistry." McGraw-Hill (Blackiston), New York.

Colowick, S. P., and Kaplan, N. O., eds. (1957). "Methods in Enzymology," Vol. IV, pp. 425–914. Academic Press, New York.

Comar, C. L. (1955). "Radioisotopes in Biology and Agriculture." McGraw-Hill, New York.

Hevesy, G. (1948). "Radioactive Indicators." Wiley (Interscience), New York.

Kamen, M. D. (1957). "Isotopic Tracers in Biology." Academic Press, New York.

Quimby, E. H. (1962–1963). "Radioactive Isotopes in Medicine and Biology." Lea & Febiger, Philadelphia.

Rothchild, S., ed. (1963). "Advances in Tracer Methodology." Plenum Press, New York.

1

Some Physics and Chemistry

1. The Structure of Matter; Isotopes

The smallest particle to which matter can be reduced by chemical means is the atom. But atoms can be broken down further by powerful physical forces into smaller units. The core of the atom, containing almost all its mass (though occupying only a small fraction of its volume), is the nucleus. Around it circle, like planets round the sun, the almost weightless electrons. The nucleus consists of protons, bearing a positive electric charge, and an approximately equal number of neutrons, with the same mass as the proton, but without electric charge.

The electrons circling the nucleus are negatively charged, and are exactly equal in number to the protons within the nucleus, thereby producing an electrically uncharged total atom. All chemical and biological properties of the atom are due to the electrons, especially their number and the way their orbits around the nucleus are arranged. This number, which of course is also the number of protons within the nucleus, is different for every element, determines its properties, and is called the "atomic number" of that element. It ranges from 1, for hydrogen (1 proton, 1 electron), to 100 and over, for the transuranium elements. However, nuclei contain, besides the protons, also neutrons. These, being electrically uncharged, are not balanced by electrons, but contribute to the mass of the whole atom. Therefore, neutrons in the nucleus exert no effect on the chemical properties of the atom, but only contribute to its weight (mass). They are equal in mass to the protons. The number of protons and neutrons combined, making up the total mass of the nucleus, is called the mass number, and can range from 1 for hydrogen (1 proton) to 244 for Californium. From what has been said it is obvious that, if the number of protons in an atom is kept constant but the number of neutrons is varied, the chemical behavior of the atom will remain the same, but the atomic weight will change. Atoms of differing weights (i.e., differing number of neutrons), but identical chemical properties (i.e., identical number of protons and hence of electrons), are called isotopes. Most elements occurring in nature are mixtures of isotopes; the nuclei of their atoms have a certain number of protons, but vary in the number of neutrons, although one particular isotope usually predominates. Thus, oxygen exists principally as $_8O^{16}$, where the subscript 8 gives the number of protons in the nucleus, balanced by an equal number of electrons and fixing the chemical properties of oxygen (atomic number). The superscript 16 denotes the total number of particles, protons and neutrons, in the nucleus, giving the weight of the atom (mass number). It follows, of course, that the mass number minus the atomic number equals the number of neutrons. Natural oxygen contains also a very small amount of isotopes $_8O^{17}$ and $_8O^{18}$, the first with one and the second with two extra neutrons in the nucleus. Natural carbon is a mixture of $_6C^{12}$ with small amounts of $_6C^{13}$ (1%) and $_6C^{14}$ (10^{-10}%), and hydrogen, $_1H^1$, with $_1H^2$ and $_1H^3$. In fact, the heavy isotope of hydrogen, often called deuterium, $_1H^2$ (1 proton and 1 neutron in the nucleus, balanced by 1 orbiting electron), is manufactured by an electrolytic enrichment process applied to ordinary water.

However, enrichment procedures of the minute fractions

of the naturally occurring isotopes are not usually feasible, and the atomic reactor has provided an easy means for the production of artificial isotopes. From what has been said above, it would only be necessary to take an atom and add a neutron to its nucleus, to obtain an isotopic atom. This is exactly what is done. However, the process is somewhat complex and needs further explanation.

The nucleus of the atom contains almost all the weight of the atom, but occupies only a small fraction of its volume. The nucleus, therefore, has an exceedingly high density, about 100 million tons per cubic centimeter. To compress matter to such an extent requires forces not found outside the nucleus, forces which act only over the short range comprised by the nuclear diameter. If a new neutron were to be introduced into a nucleus, it would have to be captured and bound by these forces, and an equivalent, very large amount of energy would be liberated. This energy is something of a magnitude quite different in scale from the energies of chemical or biological reactions, and can be calculated by means of Einstein's theory of the equivalence of mass and energy. The neutron plus the nucleus *before* interaction would have a greater mass than the neutron plus the nucleus *after* the neutron has entered, and combined with, the nucleus. In other words, the sum of the parts after combination weighs less than the constituent parts separately. The difference in mass is equivalent to the "binding energy," the force binding the entering neutron to the other particles of the nucleus. This energy is liberated in the form of radiation in the process of binding the new neutron. This is, of course, also the amount of energy needed to tear apart a nucleus and remove a neutron from it.

Take the simplest example: the fusion of a neutron (n) with a proton (p). A neutron emerging from an atomic reactor is captured by the nucleus of a hydrogen atom, and thereby forms the nucleus of a new atom, a hydrogen isotope. This isotope is deuterium, and its nucleus is known as a deuteron (d). The energy liberated in the course of capture is in the form of γ-radiation (a type of radiation similar to X-rays). This nuclear reaction is symbolized in the form:

$$n + p \rightarrow d + \gamma$$

The energy released is 2.18 million electron volts, about 1 million times more energy than is liberated in a chemical reaction. This enormous energy is equivalent to the difference in mass between the sum of the mass of the neutron and proton determined separately, and that of the neutron and proton measured after combination (the deuteron).

After neutron capture, the newly formed nucleus can be either stable or unstable. If stable, the new isotopic element will be distinguishable only by its atomic weight from the normally occurring atoms. If unstable, the new nucleus will sooner or later fall apart again, and in so doing will emit radiation. Hence, unstable (or radioactive) isotopes are detectable both by their different weight and by the emission of radiation.

2. RADIOACTIVITY

The interaction between a proton and a neutron produces a more stable arrangement of nuclear particles than between two protons or two neutrons. Therefore, the most stable nuclear configuration is one of an equal number of protons and neutrons; for instance, naturally occurring oxygen, $_8O^{16}$: 8 protons and 8 neutrons; or carbon, $_6C^{12}$: 6 protons and 6 neutrons. But there is also the stable carbon isotope, $_6C^{13}$: 6 protons and 7 neutrons. Obviously, one more neutron is still tolerated without disintegration of the nucleus. But take the carbon isotope $_6C^{14}$: 6 protons and 8 neutrons—the resulting nucleus has too many neutrons compared to the protons and falls apart, or disintegrates, thereby giving off radiation. This is the radioactive isotope of carbon which is of great importance in biochemical research. It disintegrates not by loss of a neutron (this would require a large energy input), but by transformation of one of the neutrons in its nucleus into a proton. Thereby the radioactive carbon isotope, $_6C^{14}$ (6 protons, 8 neutrons), becomes the stable nitrogen isotope, $_7N^{14}$ (7 protons, 7 neutrons; a stable nuclear configuration). In the conversion of a neutron to a proton, a practically weightless electron, carrying a negative electric charge, is given off. The original neutron was uncharged; with loss of a weightless negative charge, the newly formed particle will be a proton (same mass with positive charge). The escaping electron carries with it a packet of energy. This is so because a more stable configuration has been achieved and therefore "binding energy" can be released. The escaping electron is called a β-particle, and the radiation that it forms is β-radiation.

Similarly, isotopes exist which have more protons than neutrons, and will revert to a more stable configuration of an equal number of each by release of a positron. This is a practically weightless particle bearing a positive charge.

In general, radioactivity of isotopes is caused by nuclear instability, and emission of radiation by the process of return to a more stable state.

3. ENERGY OF RADIATION

Sometimes the nucleus which results from the emission of the β-ray is not yet in the most stable energy state. More radiation is liberated, of a kind similar to X-rays, called γ-radiation, as a transition (a sort of rearrangement) of the remaining nuclear particles takes place from a higher to a lower energy level. One then speaks of a "decay scheme" (the unstable, radioactive nucleus "decays"). This describes the sequence of events following the disintegration of a nucleus: the emission of β- or γ-radiation, or both, and their energies. It has been found that β- and γ-radiation emitted by different isotopes has different energies. These are expressed in million electron volts (Mev.) per disintegrating atom (Table I).

As will be seen later, for biological work it is important to choose an isotope emitting radiation of the right energy for the particular job. It is, for instance, possible to produce labeled chromosomes (see Chap. V, Sect. II-4) with a carbon isotope, C^{14}, or a hydrogen isotope, H^3. The former emits β-radiation of medium energy (0.155 Mev.), the latter β-radiation of very low energy (0.019 Mev.). When exposed to photographic film, the carbon isotope blackens many silver grains of the photographic emulsion, with each disintegration, because of the higher energy of its radiation. The energy of H^3-radiation, on the other hand, is so low that each disintegrating atom of the isotope causes the blackening of one silver grain only. Therefore, the picture obtained by exposure to film of a C^{14}-labeled chromosome looks blurred; from a H^3-labeled chromosome it appears sharply focused.

As was mentioned, β-particles are electrons and therefore practically weightless, negatively charged, and moving with high velocities. Being charged, they produce ions when they collide and interact with matter (an atom which has gained or lost an electron and bears an electric charge becomes an ion). It is through this ion production that radiation can be detected. After collision, the particles are deflected; they are scattered and trace an erratic way through matter, until their energy is dissipated through ion production. A β-particle from C^{14} with a maximum energy of 0.15 Mev., for instance, produces about 5,000 ions in air before it comes to rest.

Gamma-radiation consists of photons (quanta of electromagnetic radiation resembling X-rays) of high energy, moving at the speed of light. Being uncharged, they interact much less easily with matter. Therefore, they have an enormously greater penetrating power than β-radiation.

TABLE I

RADIATION ENERGIES OF VARIOUS RADIOACTIVE ISOTOPES[a]

Atomic number	Symbol and mass number	Half-life[b]		Radiation characteristics[c]
1	H^3	12	y	β^- 0.017–0.019 No γ
6	C^{14}	5700	y	No γ, β^- 0.155
9	F^{18}	112	m	β^+ 0.60 (80%), 0.95 (20%)
11	Na^{24}	14.8	h	β^- 1.39 γ 1.38, 2.76
15	P^{32}	14.30	d	β^- 1.71 No γ
16	S^{35}	87.1	d	β^- 0.1670 No γ
17	Cl^{36}	4.4×10^5 y		β^- 0.73, β^+ K
19	K^{42}	12.4	h	β^- 3.58, 2.04 γ 1.51
20	Ca^{45}	152	d	β^- 0.260 No γ
24	Cr^{51}	26.5	d	K, no β^+ γ 0.32
26	Fe^{59}	47	d	β^- 0.26, 0.460 γ 1.10, 1.30
27	Co^{60}	5.3	y	β^- 0.308 γ 1.115, 1.317
29	Cu^{64}	12.8	h	K β^- 0.571 β^+ 0.657 γ (1.35)
30	Zn^{65}	250	d	K, γ 1.11 β^+ 0.32
34	Se^{75}	125	d	K γ 0.08, 0.10, 0.12, 0.14, 0.27, 0.28, 0.40
35	Br^{82}	34	h	β^- 0.465 γ 0.547, 0.787, 1.35
38	Sr^{90}	25	y	β^- 0.61 No γ
53	I^{131}	8.0	d	β^- 0.605, 0.250 γ 0.164, 0.177, 0.284, 0.364, 0.625

TABLE I (*Continued*)

Atomic number	Symbol and mass number	Half-life[b]		Radiation characteristics[c]
56	Ba[140]	12.8	d	β^- 1.05, 0.34
				γ 0.54

[a] From M. D. Kamen, "Radioactive Tracers in Biology," p. 382. Academic Press, New York, 1951.

[b] Abbreviations: y, years; d, days; h, hours; m, minutes.

[c] β^-, negative beta particles; β^+, positive beta particles; γ, gamma rays; K, orbital electron capture. Figures denote maximum values of energies of radiation in million electron volts.

However, they ultimately also collide with matter and produce ions. Their path in air is many meters long.

4. DECAY OF RADIOACTIVITY

If the nucleus of a radioactive atom is highly unstable, it will disintegrate rapidly; if less unstable, more slowly. The radioactivity decays as the nucleus becomes transformed into a stable configuration. This decay is a random process. Take a test tube full of radioactive atoms: no chemical or physical means can make one atom contained in this test tube disintegrate rather than another. Which atom will decay at any moment is a matter of chance— hence the random, uneven response of the Geiger counter with which we are all familiar: click—click—clickclickclick —click—clickclick. As more and more atoms in the test tube emit their radioactivity and become stable, fewer and fewer radioactive atoms remain. This decay can be expressed graphically in a decay curve (Fig. 1), where the logarithms of the units of radioactivity are plotted against time, giving a straight line. The "half-life" is defined as the time when one half have decayed (Fig. 1). Half-lives of commonly used isotopes are given in Table I. It is obvious that, for biological work, isotopes with long half-lives are essential. Fortunately, the most important of them, radioactive carbon, C^{14}, has a half-life of 5,000 years, radio-active hydrogen (tritium), H^3, of 12 years, and radioactive sulfur, S^{35}, of 87 days. If one were to use the iodine isotope I^{128} (half-life, 25 min.), instead of the more common I^{131} (half-life 8 days), one would find after 4 hours that 99.9% of the isotope had decayed to stable xenon.

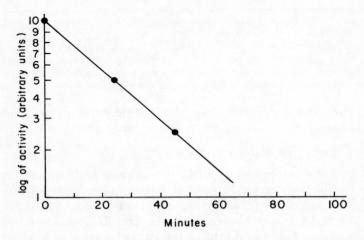

FIG. 1. Decay curve for the isotope C^{11} ($\tau_{1/2} = 21.0$ min.). It will be noted that the intensity of radioactivity drops a factor of 2 every 21 min. Ordinates are plotted on log scale; $\tau_{1/2}$ denotes half-life. [From M. D. Kamen, "Isotopic Tracers in Biology," p. 15. Academic Press, New York, 1957.]

When using a short-lived isotope in a biological experiment, a correction must be made for the loss of radioactivity by decay during the time it takes to carry out the experiment. This can be done by calculation on the basis of the known decay curve for the particular isotope (e.g., Fig. 1). More commonly, a standard sample of the isotope is kept in storage during the whole time of the experiment; the per cent loss in radioactivity which it shows is the same as that lost by the experimental samples through decay during the time of the experiment.

5. Production of Isotopes

By far the most useful and efficient means of isotope production is the atomic reactor, providing a rich source of slow neutrons. Neutrons are uncharged particles and therefore lose little energy by interaction with electrons or repulsion by nuclei. They can enter nuclei more readily than charged particles. They have to be slowed to low energies (by "moderators" such as paraffin wax or water) so that they linger near nuclei for a longer time than fast neutrons would. They thereby acquire an increased chance of being captured by nuclei.

The simplest form of isotope production is neutron capture, that is, entry of a neutron with simultaneous emission of γ-radiation. The neutron which enters and the γ-ray which leaves the nucleus are both uncharged, hence the net result is a change in atomic mass but not in atomic number. Another way of saying this is that the weight of the atom increases, but its chemical properties remain the same. For example, a radioactive isotope of sodium is produced by capture of a slow neutron from the atomic reactor:

$$_{11}Na^{23} + \quad _{0}n^{1} \quad \rightarrow \quad _{11}Na^{24} + \quad \gamma$$

| Normal sodium | Neutron | Radio-active sodium | Radiation |

As discussed in a previous section (Chap. I, Sect. 2), neutron capture increases the ratio of neutrons to protons in the nucleus. The new atom is unstable and, to right the balance again, disintegrates. A neutron is transformed into a proton, with concomitant emission of β-radiation. In this way, radioactive sodium disintegrates again in the way depicted below:

$$_{11}Na^{24} \rightarrow \quad _{12}Mg^{24} \quad + \quad \beta^{-}$$

| Radio-active sodium | Stable magnesium | Radiation |

Neutron capture with γ-emission is not the most useful way of producing isotopes. In the above sample, radioactive sodium, the product of the nuclear reaction, is chemically indistinguishable from the starting material, normal sodium. The radioactive element cannot be separated by chemical means from the residual normal element. This is a distinct disadvantage, as it results in isotopic material of low specific activity (radioactivity per unit weight).

A much more useful method of isotope manufacture consists in the transmutations brought about by reaction with neutrons. The most important is the formation of radioactive carbon, thus:

$$_7N^{14} \; + \; _0n^1 \rightarrow \; _6C^{14} \; + \; _1H^1$$
Normal		Radio-	Proton
nitrogen		active	
		carbon	

In practice, a nitrogen-containing compound such as ammonium nitrate or beryllium nitride, packed in aluminum cans, is lowered into the atomic pile where it comes into contact and reacts with a flow of neutrons slowed by moderators. The resulting product is dissolved in sulfuric acid and hydrogen peroxide, and the gas obtained, consisting mainly of radioactive carbon dioxide, and methane, is swept out. The methane is oxidized to carbon dioxide, and all of this gas is made to react with barium hydroxide. Radioactive barium carbonate precipitates. This compound is then used as starting material for the synthesis of a large variety of labeled organic compounds (Chap. I, Sect. 7). In this way, 100% isotopic carbon could be obtained, though in practice it is diluted to about 16% isotope concentration, on account of the danger of radiation decomposition (to be discussed later in this chapter).

Radioactive carbon disintegrates by the scheme:

$$_6C^{14} \; \rightarrow \; _7N^{14} \; + \; \beta^-$$
Radio-	Normal	
active	nitrogen	
carbon		

Radioactive sulfur and phosphorus are made by exactly the same procedure:

$$_{17}Cl^{35} + _{0}n^{1} \rightarrow {} _{16}S^{35} + _{1}H^{1}; \qquad _{16}S^{32} + _{0}n^{1} \rightarrow {} _{15}P^{32} + _{1}H^{1}$$

Normal	Radio-	Normal	Radio-
chlorine	active	sulfur	active
	sulfur		phosphorus

The disintegration reactions are:

$$_{16}S^{35} \rightarrow {} _{17}Cl^{35} + \beta^{-}; \qquad _{15}P^{32} \rightarrow {} _{16}S^{32} + \beta^{-}$$

Radioactive hydrogen is made somewhat differently. Lithium is irradiated by slow neutrons, and an α-particle (the nucleus of a helium atom) is given off:

$$_{3}Li^{6} + _{0}n^{1} \rightarrow {} _{1}H^{3} + _{2}He^{4}$$

Normal lithium   Radioactive hydrogen α-Particle

Radioactive iodine (I^{131}) is found amongst the fission products of uranium. Upon disintegration, it emits both β- and γ-radiation.

There are some isotopes that cannot be produced by nuclear reactions with neutrons. Instead, electrically charged particles must be endowed with sufficient energy in a particle accelerator (cyclotron) to cause them to enter nuclei and participate in nuclear reactions. These particles are ions (atoms with an electron missing or an extra electron, therefore bearing an electric charge). When approaching a nucleus, ions suffer energy losses due to repulsion by the positively charged nucleus, and must approach with enormous energy to overcome this repulsion. For instance, radioactive sodium can be made by accelerating deuterons (positively charged ions of deuterium, a stable hydrogen isotope), and causing them to strike a magnesium target.

$$_{12}Mg^{24} + _{1}H^{2} \rightarrow {} _{11}Na^{22} + _{2}He^{4}$$

Normal magnesium   Deuteron   Radioactive sodium α-Particle

6. MEASUREMENT OF RADIOACTIVITY AND OF STABLE ISOTOPE CONCENTRATION

A detailed discussion of the various instruments used for radioactivity assay is outside the scope of this book, and will be treated separately in another volume of this series. However, mention must be made, at least in outline, of the more important types that are most often used in practice.

Devices for measuring radioactivity can be conveniently divided into categories according to the type of material for which they are generally used: (*1*) ionization chambers, for gases; (*2*) Geiger-Mueller and proportional counters, for solids; (*3*) liquid scintillation counters, for liquids and solutions; (*4*) crystal scintillation counters, for liquids and solids emitting high-energy radiation. Each device can, of course, be adapted for materials in another state of matter—radioactive solids can be assayed in ionization chambers, etc.; but the categories listed above are those generally found most convenient.

(*1*) The radioactive gas in an ionization chamber produces ions by collision with the gas molecules. These ions are collected on electrodes at a relatively low potential. The current thereby produced is amplified by an electrometer device (vibrating reed electrometer), and can be read on a galvanometer. The current produced is proportional to the average rate of ion production, and therefore to the radioactivity of the gas.

(*2*) Radiation emitted by a solid sample close to a Geiger-Mueller or proportional counter causes ionization of the gas (helium and isobutane) with which the counter is filled. The high voltage applied to the electrodes in the counter leads to multiplication of these ions several thousands of times, and ultimately to a discharge of the potential. This discharge is registered as one "count" on a scaling device. Thus, these counters measure each β- or γ-ray entering the counter separately. The magnitude of the discharge produced in the proportional counter, in addition, is proportional to the energy of the entering radiation.

(3) In the liquid scintillation counter, the radioactive material is intimately mixed (in solution) with an organic compound which has the property of emitting flashes of light on interaction with radiation. The light so produced is "seen" by a photoelectric cell. The cell thereupon releases electrons which are amplified and registered on a scaling device. Each flash of light, and hence each discharge, corresponds to the disintegration of an isotopic atom, and its intensity to the energy of the ray emitted. This type of counter is best suited, in fact the only one available, to assay satisfactorily the weak β-radiation of radioactive hydrogen (tritium).

(4) The crystal scintillation counter operates on the same principle as the liquid scintillation counter, except that the radiation coming from the sample here strikes a crystal of sodium iodide containing traces of thallium iodide. This has the property of emitting flashes of light corresponding to the radiation which strikes it. It is used principally to determine the radioactivity of γ-emitters (e.g., I^{131}).

An array of accessory instruments is available in addition to the above four types of counter. Rate meters are Geiger-Mueller counters which register the *rate* of disintegration of a given isotope. These have been adapted to a small, battery-operated form serving as laboratory monitors. Paper strip scanners are Geiger-Mueller counters modified to scan paper chromatograms (see Chap. V, Sec. II-1) and register the spots on the paper which are radioactive, as well as indicate the amount of radioactivity in them. Finally, there is the electronic equipment necessary to supply the high voltage to the counters and register and time the discharges (scalers and timers).

Measurement of the concentration of stable isotopes is

much more difficult, and also less sensitive, than assay of radioactive isotopes, since it depends only on differences in atomic weight. Therefore, in biology, stable isotopes are used only when no radioactive ones are available for a particular job; for instance, the heavy isotopes of nitrogen, N^{15}, and oxygen, O^{18}. There is one exception. Because of the so-called "isotope effect" (see Chap. IV, Sect. I-1), it is sometimes necessary in biochemistry to employ "carrier-free" isotopes. As was explained (Chap. I, Sect. 5), it is not possible to prepare organic compounds consisting only of the radioactive isotope of carbon (C^{14}) without admixture of nonradioactive, normal C^{12} as "carrier." Radiation decomposition would render such a compound totally unstable (Chap. I, Sect. 9). However, with the stable isotope C^{13}, carrier-free isotopic organic compounds can be prepared without fear of radiation damage. Furthermore, for experiments with human subjects, radioactive isotopes are not usually employed because of the harmful effect of radiation released within the body. Stable isotopes are quite harmless.

The most common method for assay of stable isotope concentration is the mass spectrometer. The sample is converted to a gaseous form, the gas is ionized, and the ions are accelerated by an electric field. The stream of ions is then deflected by a magnetic field: the angle of deflection varies with the weight of the ions, so that the heavier isotopic ions arrive at a different target than the lighter, normal ions. At the target, the concentrations of the respective ions are measured and registered.

7. SYNTHESIS OF RADIOACTIVE COMPOUNDS

Isotopic compounds in biological work can be used as simple salts for which no elaborate means of synthesis are needed, for instance, radioactive sodium chloride, $Na^{24}Cl$, in studies of ion transport, or calcium chloride, $Ca^{45}Cl$, in experiments on bone formation. However, carbon and hydrogen isotopes, to be of any use, must be incorporated into the organic compounds in the form in which they normally appear in nature. To synthesize complex naturally occurring organic compounds from isotopic carbon dioxide or isotopic water or hydrogen (the raw materials available from the isotope manufacturing process), requires elaborate chemical processes and intricate equipment, which cannot be described here in detail (Calvin, 1949; Catch, 1961). The problem is not simply one of using known chemical syntheses and putting isotopic materials into the mixture in place of the normal materials. The limitations are the following: work must be done on a small scale, usually in the millimole range (1 millimole of the amino acid glycine, for instance, weighs 75 mg. or about 0.003 oz.). This is done not only in order to conserve expensive isotopic material, but also because it is essential to maintain a high specific activity (i.e., radioactivity per unit weight), in other words, a high concentration of isotopic compared to normal atoms. It would be easy enough to dilute a small amount of radioactive starting material with a large quantity of normal, nonradioactive compound, and in this way increase the scale of operations. But this would defeat the aim of the synthesis. One might end up, it is true, with a large sample, but of such low specific activity that it would be quite useless. For in the biological experiment the isotopic compound suffers a great deal of further dilution by normal material, until in the end it would become undetectable among the masses of nonradioactive atoms around it.

The second limitation is that yields of reactions employed must be high. This, again, is done to conserve isotope and also to minimize impurities. If, as an example, in a reaction the yield is 20%, then the product must be extracted from 80% of impurities. It is obvious that the danger of contamination of the product with impurities will be acute. It would be much less so if the product constituted 80% and the impurities 20%. This problem of radiochemical purity is especially troublesome in isotopic syntheses. The great advantage gained in sensitivity by use of radioisotopes has its obverse in the great havoc that a minute impurity can make of a biochemical experiment. Consider, for instance, the use of labeled proline which is injected into a rat in order to study its conversion to hydroxyproline. Suppose the sample contained 0.1% of hydroxyproline as an impurity, a quantity not easily detectable by ordinary chemical methods. If a dose of 5 mg. of proline, containing 5,000,000 counts per minute (c.p.m.) of radioactivity, is administered to a rat, it will contain the miniscule amount of 0.005 mg. of labeled hydroxyproline (5,000 c.p.m.). If the blood of the animal is collected shortly after injection and analyzed, it will be found to have in it a good proportion of these 5,000 c.p.m. of the labeled hydroxyproline impurity. The erroneous conclusion would be that, upon injection of proline into an animal, free hydroxyproline is formed rapidly and appears in the blood stream.

The criteria of radiochemical purity must be rigorously applied to the end products of isotopic syntheses. These criteria are: maintenance of specific activity through various purification steps, degradation and derivative preparation, isotope dilution, and chromatography. They will be further discussed (Chapter V, Sect. I-3), since they apply as much to isolation of compounds from biological systems as to end products of isotopic syntheses.

Another limitation in isotopic syntheses is the fact that, since all the compounds have to be made from carbon dioxide, most of the intermediates are compounds of low molecular weight and, therefore, usually volatile. Carbon dioxide itself is a gas. Therefore, volatilization in the course of synthesis causes hazards of contamination and might endanger health, besides leading to waste of isotope. Hence, the work must be done in completely closed systems. This can be achieved by carrying out all operations on a "vacuum line" (Fig. 2), a system of glass tubes evacuated to 10^{-3} mm. Hg by a mercury diffusion pump. It permits the radiochemist to work with small amounts of volatile materials, to make quantitative transfers from one vessel to another, and to measure continuously, by means

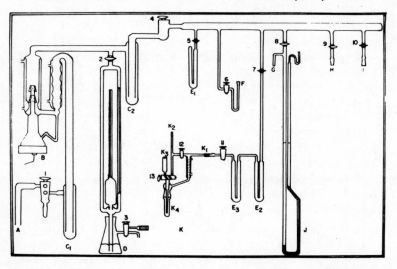

FIG. 2. High vacuum line in conjunction with wet combustion apparatus. A, Fore pump; B, mercury diffusion pump; C_1, C_2, E_1, E_2, E_3 and G traps; D, McLeod gauge; $1'$–13, stopcocks; J, manometer; K, wet combustion apparatus. [From M. T. H. Ragab and J. P. McCollum, *Weeds* **9**, 72 (1961).]

of a manometer, the extent of the reaction. Many liquids (water, alcohol, ether, acetic acid) are gases at the very low pressures inside the vacuum line, and diffuse rapidly, being moved by their own kinetic energy. They can, therefore, be readily transferred from one tube E_3 (Fig. 2), to another E_2. This is done by warming the tube E_3 and cooling tube E_2 with an extremely cold liquid from the outside (liquid nitrogen, boiling point $-196°C$). To give an example: $C^{14}O_2$ is bled into the vacuum line at K_1 (Fig. 2)

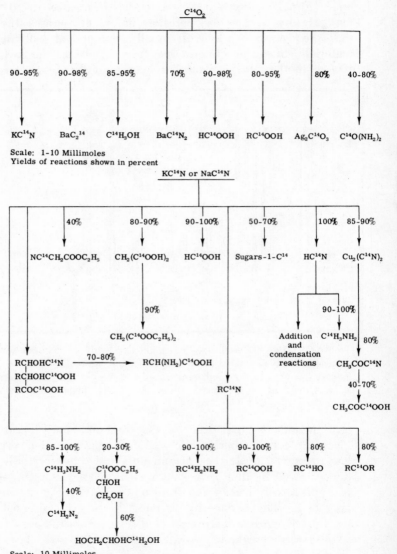

Scale: 1-10 Millimoles
Yields of reactions shown in percent

Scale: 10 Millimoles
Yields of reactions shown in percent

and trapped in tube E_3, by cooling. Methylmagnesium iodide is placed in a tube attached at H, which is then cooled and evacuated. The cooling agent is then removed from tube E_3 so that the radioactive carbon dioxide gas distills from E_3 into the tube at H, where it reacts to form ultimately C^{14}-labeled acetic acid, which can again be distilled out. For the chemically minded, a flow sheet is given (Fig. 3) that illustrates the ingenious syntheses devised to build up complex labeled molecules for use in biology, starting with carbon dioxide.

8. PREPARATION OF TRITIUM-LABELED COMPOUNDS

Similar syntheses have been worked out for labeled hydrogen (H^3, tritium), to prepare complex tritium-labeled organic compounds.

The advantage of tritium labeling lies in the fact that higher specific activities can be obtained than with carbon: carrier-free tritium has 57.5 curies per milliatom, carbon only 0.054. This is due to the much shorter half-life of tritium, and therefore its greater rate of decay.

Another way exists for labeling organic compounds with tritium, recently discovered by Wilzbach. It dispenses with the slow step-by-step building up of the complex molecule from small labeled building blocks. This method is especially suited for the rapid, easy preparation of radioactive drugs or food additives and dyes, which must undergo metabolic tests to satisfy the requirements of the Food and Drug Laws (see Chap. VI, Sect. I-3). The unlabeled compound, consisting of the completed molecule itself, obtained sometimes from biological sources (an enzyme has been so labeled), or simply by normal, large-scale synthesis,

FIG. 3. Schemes for the syntheses of C^{14}-labeled compounds starting with $C^{14}O_2$. Numbers refer to per cent yields in reactions. [From R. F. Nystrom, *in* "Expanding the Utilization of Radioisotopes" (J. H. Rust, ed.), p. 27, M. I. T. Press, Cambridge, Massachusetts, 1958.]

is finely powdered and kept in a tube in contact with highly radioactive tritium gas. The energy of the β-particles emitted in close contact with the organic compound is sufficient to break some of the carbon-hydrogen bonds, and in some cases the bonds reform with tritium substituting for hydrogen. Of course, labeled impurities are also produced, and purification procedures and purity checks must be even more rigorous than for C^{14} syntheses. Furthermore, oxygen-hydrogen bonds are sometimes much weaker than carbon-hydrogen or carbon-carbon bonds, so that a tritium atom, when bound to an oxygen atom, could be lost merely in the course of dissolving the labeled compound. Therefore, such tritium atoms must be removed or "exchanged out" of the material before use, by dissolving the compound in water, and removing the water into which the tritium has exchanged from the compound.

It has recently been found by Nystrom that tritium, instead of substituting for hydrogen atoms, will *add* to unsaturated positions of organic compounds, thus producing an entirely different substance from that which had been originally exposed to the tritium gas and which it had been the intention to label. Often these new materials are difficult to separate from the intended labeled compound. Sometimes highly tritiated impurities are formed in trace amounts, so small that they cannot be detected and separated from the mass of unlabeled material with which they occur. Much confusion has resulted from inadequate purification, and from use of the wrong labeled compound in metabolism studies. The importance of quite exceptionally high standards in the purification of tritium-labeled compounds prepared by the Wilzbach method is therefore obvious.

9. PREPARATIVE BIOSYNTHESIS

An easy, cheap, and rapid method for the synthesis of C^{14}-labeled compounds is simply to let plants or microorganisms do the work for you: this is called preparative biosynthesis. Take a large leaf, put it in a glass chamber filled with C^{14}-labeled carbon dioxide, and shine a strong light upon it. The leaf, in spite of being separated from the plant, continues to photosynthesize, and incorporates $C^{14}O_2$ into sucrose, starch, and other compounds. After a few hours, the labeled products can be isolated. The advantage lies in the fact that very complicated organic compounds can be made radioactive very rapidly, using only labeled carbon dioxide as a precursor. Furthermore, many compounds occurring in nature are in a particular molecular configuration ("optically active"), which is difficult to achieve in the laboratory. Yet it is just these optically active forms that are of most value in biological experiment. In preparative biosynthesis the optically active material is immediately and easily obtained, in fact, is the only form that is produced. The drawback of the method is that the compounds formed are "uniformly labeled." Since the labeled CO_2 enters all the reactions taking place in the plants, all carbon atoms of every compound will have some label on it. This does not mean that every carbon atom in the compound is labeled equally, but simply that every carbon atom has *some* radioactivity. If it is the aim of the biological experiment to trace the molecule as a whole, the uniformly labeled material is adequate. However, biochemists usually wish to trace *parts* of molecules, or single carbon atoms, through a series of metabolic reactions. For this purpose, it is greatly to be preferred that the atom under investigation be the only one labeled, and therefore uniformly labeled substances would be useless.

Rigorous purification is, of course, of paramount importance in preparative biosynthesis. It is to be expected that, together with the desired compound, several *closely similar* compounds will be formed in the plant. Their very similarity makes purification difficult and can lead to unsuspected labeled impurities.

In practice, preparative biosynthesis has been most rewarding in the preparation of uniformly labeled sugars by plants, and amino acids by algae. A large number of labeled drugs has been produced by the Argonne National Laboratory in their "Isotope Farms," where drug-forming plants are grown in sealed greenhouses supplied with labeled carbon dioxide. In this manner, labeled digitoxin is made by growing *Digitalis purpurea* in $C^{14}O_2$. Labeled blood serum albumin can be made by feeding animals a mixture of labeled amino acids (derived from algae), and extracting the albumin from the serum after the animal has incorporated the C^{14}-amino acids into it.

10. RADIATION DECOMPOSITION

When highly radioactive compounds are stored on the shelf, they can "spoil" by a process known as "radiation decomposition." The higher the concentration of C^{14} in the sample, the higher the specific activity, and the greater will be the number of β-particles with maximum energy of 0.154 million electron volts given off per minute. This radiation has enough energy to break chemical bonds (bond breaking, followed by formation of new bonds, is the principle of the Wilzbach method; see Chap. I, Sect. 8). The range of specific activity of compounds normally synthesized is generally 1–10 millicuries (mc.) per millimole. Decomposition on storage begins to be serious at 20 mc. per mmole, depending, of course, on the position in the molecule of the radioactive atom, and its surrounding atoms. Methanol, $C^{14}H_3OH$ (8 mc./mmole), is destroyed to the extent of 19% upon 2 years' storage. Choline, $(C^{14}H_3)_3$ $\overset{+}{N}CH_2CH_2OH$ (1.8 mc./mmole), is destroyed to the extent of 63% in 1 year. Carbon-nitrogen bonds are the most sensitive to radiation decomposition. Decomposition can be prevented to some extent by storage of the labeled compound in solution, or adsorbed to filter paper, so that a great proportion of the radiation is absorbed by the solvent or paper before it can do any harm.

REFERENCES

Calvin, M. (1949). "Isotopic Carbon." Wiley, New York.
Catch, J. R. (1961). "Carbon-14 Compounds." Butterworths, London.

II

Units of Radioactivity
and of Stable Isotopes

1. UNITS OF RADIOACTIVITY; PARAMETERS

A brief definition of the units generally used in work with isotopes is in order at this point. For radioactive isotopes, the units are defined by the following three parameters:

(*a*) The energy of the radiation emitted by the isotope.

(*b*) The number of radioactive atoms present in the sample to be considered.

(*c*) The half-life of the isotope; this determines the rate at which the given number of isotopic atoms disintegrates per unit time.

(*a*): The unit of "electron volt" defines the energy of radiation, as was explained (Chap. I, Sect. 3).

(*a*, *b*, and *c*): The unit which describes the effect of radiation, and therefore combines all three of the above parameters, is the "roentgen" (r) (it will be described in Chapter III).

(*b* and *c*): The unit of radioactivity most useful in biological work defines the rate of disintegration occurring in a given sample of material, and therefore refers to the number of isotopic atoms in the sample as well as to their disintegration rate. It is defined as the "curie," or the radioactivity contained in 1 gm. of radium. Experimentally, in this amount of radium 3.7×10^{10} disintegrations per second (d.p.s.) were found to occur. This figure is now taken as the fundamental unit of radioactivity. It is more commonly used as the millicurie (mc.), 3.7×10^7 d.p.s., or microcurie (μc.), 3.7×10^4 d.p.s., the latter being 2.2×10^6 disintegrations per minute. Since most counting devices, such as internal gas flow counters and proportional counters (see Chap. II, Sect. 6), have the property of detecting (and therefore registering or counting) about 50% of all the disintegrations of a sample, one can say as a rough approximation that 1 μc. gives about 1 million counts per minute (c.p.m.).

As was explained, the curie combines parameters (b) and (c), above. Therefore, if a sample of C^{14} is said to have 1 μc. of radioactivity, it would have to contain many more isotopic atoms than a sample of H^3 (tritium) of 1 μc. This is because the microcurie defines the rate of disintegration. For the same number of isotopic atoms, tritium has many more disintegrations per unit time, since its half-life is so much shorter (12 years) than that of C^{14} (5,000 years). This means that the unit of the curie does not define the content of isotopic atoms within a sample, if we compare different isotopes with different half-lives. However, the curie *does* define the number of isotopic atoms, if we compare different samples of the same isotope. This is the way the unit is used in practice. We speak about injecting 50 μc. of C^{14}-glycine into a rat and collecting 5 μc. of $C^{14}O_2$ from the expired breath of the rat. This means that the injected glycine contains a certain number of C^{14}-labeled molecules (about 6×10^{16}) and that the CO_2 contains 10% of that number. The number of labeled molecules in a 50-μc. sample of *tritium*-labeled glycine would be quite different and much lower (about 1×10^{14}).

2. Specific Radioactivity

The most useful unit of radioactivity is not the mc. or μc., or disintegrations per minute, or counts per minute. (The last named is no more than the number registered by the counting instrument; it is related to disintegrations per minute by a constant factor which depends on the efficiency of the instrument in registering the disintegrations.) These units merely indicate total radioactivity. They are independent of weight. One can have 1 μc. of radioactivity in a ton or in a microgram of glucose. It has therefore limited applicability, being generally used only in gross distribution studies (see Chap. VI, Sect. I). As soon as the concept of *dilution* of the radioactive compound with the same material in nonradioactive form enters the situation, a much more useful unit can be applied. This is *specific activity*, radioactivity per unit weight. It can be expressed in a large number of ways: as μc., or c.p.m., or "per cent of dose" per gram, or per organ or tissue isolated, or per mole. The last named, as μc. per millimole, is the most precise, expressing radioactivity on a molecular basis. Take as an example the results of a metabolism experiment in which C^{14}-histidine was injected into a rat. Table I shows that the

TABLE I
DILUTION OF LABELED HISTIDINE INJECTED INTO THE RAT

C^{14}-histidine	Specific activity (μc. per mmole)	Total activity (μc.)
Injected into rat	429.0	69.3
Isolated from rat liver protein	11.7	4.3

injected amino acid has been diluted about 40 times with unlabeled histidine in the course of its incorporation into protein. This unlabeled histidine was derived from two sources: the amount already present in existing protein, and the amount present as free (nonprotein) histidine at the site at which the labeled amino acid was taken up into the protein. As will be shown in detail later (Chap. V, Sect. I), from the knowledge of this dilution (i.e., drop in specific activity), and of the amount of histidine originally injected, it is then possible to calculate the quantity of histidine present in the animal at the time of injection. This technique, depending entirely on the concept of specific activity, has been refined and greatly expanded for the calculation of "pool size" (amount of a particular compound present in a particular organ or animal) and "turnover" (replacement, by metabolism, excretion, and resynthesis, of a particular compound), as discussed later (Chap. VI, Sect. III).

The concept of specific activity also finds application in the purification, isolation, and estimation of compounds (a subject discussed in Chapter V).

3. SPECIFIC ACTIVITY PER MOLE

An illuminating example of the usefulness of specific activity, expressed as radioactivity per mole, is found in Table II; Glutamic acid is the result of the metabolic breakdown of histidine (Fig. 1). If the label in histidine is on the α-carbon (as shown), in which carbon, α or γ, does it

TABLE II

DEGRADATION OF GLUTAMIC ACID FROM VISCERAL PROTEIN
AFTER C[14]-HISTIDINE INJECTION[a]

Location of radioactivity	Specific activity[b] (μc. per mmole $\times 10^{-3}$)
Glutamic acid	167.5
Succinic acid, from glutamic acid	164.0
(CO$_2$ from carboxyl of succinic acid) $\times 2$	43.2 (26.3%)
Methylene carbons of succinic acid, calculated	120.8 (73.7%)

[a] From G. Wolf, *J. Biol. Chem.* **200**, 637 (1953).

[b] Specific activities refer to the samples diluted with carrier.

appear in glutamic acid? In other words, does the metabolic breakdown of histidine follow pathway A or B? This question can be clearly answered by a chemical transformation ("degradation") of the glutamic acid, isolated from the animal, to succinic acid and then to carbon dioxide, as shown in Fig. 1. From Table II it is clear that, *on a molar*

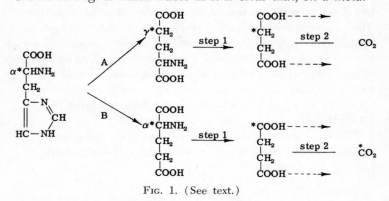

Fig. 1. (See text.)

basis, the specific activities of glutamic and succinic acids are the same, indicating that only nonradioactive carbon was lost in step *1* of the degradation, and that, mole per mole, all the radioactivity was maintained in the succinic acid from the glutamic acid. In the next degradative step, much less label was found in the resulting CO_2. Therefore, pathway B could not have been operative since here all the activity would have to appear in the CO_2. One concludes that glutamic acid must have been formed from histidine by pathway A.

Additional information can be provided by a unit of specific activity called "relative isotope concentration":

$$\frac{\mu c. \text{ per millimole of compound isolated}}{\mu c. \text{ per millimole of compound administered, per gm. body weight}}$$

This unit shows the specific activity of an isolated metabolic product in relation to the specific activity of its precursor which is fed or injected, per gram of body weight of the animal (to equalize variability of body weights). It is most useful when comparing the relation of a precursor to a product in a metabolic sequence, since it reveals the degree of dilution of the administered labeled material by un-labeled compounds of the metabolic pathway already existing in the organism. The further away the product is from the precursor in the chain of reactions, the greater will be the dilution of its radioactivity, and therefore the smaller its relative isotope concentration (R.I.C.). Thus, below, C will have a lower R.I.C. than B:

labeled
A^{***} → B^{**} → C^{*}
injected   diluted with   diluted with
            unlabeled B   unlabeled C

4. SPECIFIC ACTIVITY PER ATOM OF CARBON

In many experiments, the unit in which radioactivity is expressed is directly dependent on the technique whereby the sample to be assayed has been prepared. Compounds to be assayed are frequently combusted to carbon dioxide, which is converted to barium carbonate. This material is placed on disks ("planchets") which are inserted in a counter. If the layer of barium carbonate on the planchet exceeds a certain thickness (about 25 mg. per sq. cm.), it is known as "infinitely thick." At this thickness, the β-radia-tion emitted by the lower layers of barium carbonate on the planchet is completely absorbed ("self-absorption") by the upper layers, and does not reach the counter. Therefore, however much is loaded onto the planchet, only the barium carbonate in a constant slice of upper layer gets counted. The counts registered will be proportional not to the total amount of radioactive barium carbonate on the planchet, but to the specific activity of that upper layer. In other words, the radioactivity of an infinitely thick planchet is proportional to its specific activity. This unit (c.p.m. per sq. cm. at infinite thickness), which is a specific activity, is often used in biochemical work. This specific activity, however, is not a radioactivity per mole, but a specific activity expressed per atom of carbon, of the particular compound combusted. This is because, in the process of combustion to carbon dioxide, nonradioactive carbon from the unlabeled positions of the compound is contributed to the carbon dioxide. Specific activity, therefore, is the average of all the carbon atoms of the compound (i.e., c.p.m. per atom of carbon), rather than per mole. To convert this specific activity to a specific activity per mole of compound, one must multiply it by the number of carbon atoms in the compound. For example, benzoic acid has 7 carbon atoms per molecule. Suppose only one is labeled. When combusted to CO_2, and counted as infinitely thick barium carbonate, the radioactivity observed is 100 c.p.m. This figure is the specific activity of the benzoic acid expressed as c.p.m. per atom of carbon. The specific activity per mole is 7×100 c.p.m. per mole.

5. UNITS OF STABLE ISOTOPES

The amount of stable isotope contained in a sample is expressed on a percentage basis, as isotopic atom per cent. This is a *specific* isotope content (isotopic atoms per 100 atoms of total material), and corresponds to the specific radioactivity of radioactive isotopes.

As was mentioned, the concentration of stable isotopes in nature is relatively high, for instance 1% of C^{13} in normal carbon, so that it is necessary to include in the unit a term expressing how much of *extra* isotope there is which has been added as a tracer by the experimenter. This is the unit: atom per cent excess, the excess abundance of the isotope over its normal occurrence, expressed as a percentage. If a sample of C^{13} has been enriched to contain, say, 80% C^{13}, we say it has $80 - 1 = 79$ atom per cent excess C^{13}.

TABLE III

LABELING OF GLUTAMINE AND GLUTAMIC ACID DURING AMMONIA (99.6 ATOM % EXCESS N^{15}) INFUSION[a]

Experiment no.	Time (min.)	Tissue	Glutamine[b]			Glutamic acid[b]	
			μmoles/gm.	Amide N^{15}	α-Amino N^{15}	μmoles/gm.	N^{15}
1	8	Blood	0.57	5.7	0.87	—	—
		Brain	7.7	27.8	4.4	9.7	0.41
		Liver	2.1	16.2	3.2	1.8	15.6
2	12	Blood	0.3	12.6	3.5	—	—
		Brain	8.4	26.9	3.4	9.5	0.91
		Liver	1.0	41.8	21.9	2.7	26.7
3	25	Blood	0.32	21.4	1.8	0.08	3.1
		Brain	7.8	38.7	8.6	9.3	0.87
		Liver	0.83	28.7	5.4	1.6	13.6
4	10	Blood	0.33	8.8	1.9	0.06	4.3
		Brain	7.6	36.6	10.8	8.9	1.2
		Liver	1.4	43.7	16.4	2.0	21.9
5	15	Blood	0.44	11.8	1.9	0.08	4.8
		Brain	7.7	34.5	9.3	8.0	0.69
		Liver	2.2	38.4	9.4	2.7	27.6

[a] From Berl et al., J. Biol. Chem. **237**, 2562 (1962).
[b] All N^{15} values are expressed as atom per cent excess.

An example of the use of the unit of stable isotope is the following (Berl *et al.*, 1962): N¹⁵-ammonia (as ammonium acetate, with 99.6 atom per cent excess N^{15}) was infused into the bloodstream of an experimental animal. Brain and liver glutamic acid and glutamine were isolated. It was found (Table III) that the amino group of brain glutamine had an N^{15} content 10 times as high as that of glutamic acid. Yet it is known that glutamine is derived directly from glutamic acid, as shown below. The two compounds should therefore have the same N^{15} concentration. That they do not can be explained only by assuming the existence

Glutamic acid   Glutamine

of two separate "pools" or "compartments" for glutamic acid in brain: one, a general, large glutamic acid pool (low N^{15}); the other a small, metabolically highly active pool (high N^{15}), which provides the glutamic acid for glutamine synthesis. This compartmentalization may somehow be connected with brain function, since the glutamic acid of liver (Table III) evidently exists in a single pool only.

REFERENCE

Berl, S., Takagaki, G., Clarke, D. D., and Waelsch, H. (1962). *J. Biol. Chem.* **237**, 2562.

III

Health Hazards and Isotope Laboratory Design

1. HEALTH HAZARDS

We can detect, observe, and measure radiation by the ionization of the atoms of matter through which the radiation passes (Chap. I, Sect. 6). The interaction of certain kinds of radiation with matter results in ionization. All instruments for radioactivity assay depend on this property. The damage to our bodies inflicted by radiation is also a consequence of this ionization. Just as the energy of the radiation breaks apart and thereby ionizes the atoms in the gas filling of a Geiger-Mueller counter, and thus causes it to register a discharge, so the same energy tears up the atoms in the tissues of living organisms. The amount of damage depends, of course, on the kind and energy of radiation. It is measured by a special unit, a unit not of quantity, but of *effect* of radiation. This is the "roentgen" (r), defined as the dose of radiation which will produce ions carrying 1 electrostatic unit per cubic centimeter of air or tissue. This is equivalent to the dissipation of 93 ergs of energy per gram of tissue. It is the unit of γ- or X-ray dose. Particle radiation, such as β-radiation, is defined by the "rad," which is 100 ergs of energy absorbed per gram of absorbing tissue. In practice, the two units are equivalent if applied to tissue.

A man is killed by a radiation dose of about 1,000 r. This radiation produces 1.5×10^{15} ionizations per gram of tissue. This seems a large number, but actually represents only a few atoms per 100 million atoms of tissue which must be damaged for death to ensue. This damage, therefore, is not as easily seen as, for instance, a burn or a wound, and can be completely invisible and unnoticeable. It may lie dormant for years, as when the radiation causes tumors or damage to genetic tissue. In such cases, small doses applied frequently can act cumulatively. High doses of radiation result in more acute symptoms: destruction of blood-forming tissues, and of the lining tissues of the intestine. Cataract develops in the eyes, and skin changes occur, with malignant degeneration of many cells. However, apart from "radiation sickness" (nausea and vomiting), there is always a latent period between the formation in the tissues of ion pairs caused by the radiation, and the appearance of the symptoms.

2. RADIATION PROTECTION

In practice, daily whole-body exposure over several years of 0.03 r has resulted in no detectable immediate ill effects, though what the future holds in store for persons thus exposed is not yet known. The National Bureau of Standards (1952, 1953) has issued a Handbook which defines the *maximum permissible dose* (MPD) under different conditions, such as the age of the exposed individual, whether he is continuously exposed as a result of his occupation, the parts of his body that are exposed, etc. The maximum permissible accumulated whole-body dose equals $5(N - 18)$r, where N is the age and greater than 18.

The basic requirement for radiation protection is constant monitoring so that any excess radiation over the safe level should be instantly detected. This is done through various portable, battery-operated ionization chambers and Geiger counters ("monitors"), or by the wearing of film badges.

These are small packages of photographic film, protected from light exposure and worn attached to the clothing of the person in danger of radiation exposure. The film is sensitive to radiation and the amount of blackening can be calibrated to indicate the dose of radiation to which the person has been exposed.

Protection against the penetrating γ-rays is best achieved by lead shielding several inches thick to separate the operator and the source of radiation, be it an isotopic chemical reaction or an isotope within an experimental animal. Safe thicknesses of shielding and safe distances from the source can be readily calculated (Quimby and Feitelberg, 1962). Remote-control handling then becomes necessary, and an array of ingenious remote-control devices for chemical operations has been developed and can be bought. For small amounts of γ-radiation, distance is all that is needed, and the operator can work behind the glass door of a fume hood, wearing heavy gloves, provided the time of exposure is short. Special rooms and special hoods with highly efficient ventilation are set aside for work with γ-emitting isotopes. Operators wear special clothes and shoes which belong to the particular room.

In the vast majority of cases, biological work is done with "soft" β-emitters (C^{14} or H^3), the radiation of which is absorbed by the walls of the vessels in which they are contained. Radiation protection then boils down to confining the radioactive sample within the vessels; in other words, avoiding spills and sloppy work, especially contamination of the bodies or clothes of the workers. Radioactive samples must not enter the bodies of the operators through eating or breathing. Radioactive solutions must never be pipetted by mouth. Therefore, personal cleanliness and neatness are essential, manipulation in a well-ventilated hood is imperative, and eating or smoking in an isotope laboratory is not recommended.

"Hard" β-emitters (P^{32}), on the other hand, require some protection by shielding of the glass vessels in which they are contained, because the glass with which the β-radiation interacts, emits a kind of X-ray ("bremsstrahlung"), which can be harmful. Open, uncovered vessels are also a source of emission that one has to guard against.

3. WASTE DISPOSAL

Radioactive waste must be handled in special ways: stringent rules have been set up by the Atomic Energy Commission to prevent contamination of our environment with radioactive waste products. These materials must be returned to the producers (Oak Ridge National Laboratory), if above a certain limit, where they are buried in specially provided concrete-lined pits. The situation is somewhat easier for C^{14} and H^3 waste disposal. The total C^{14} on the earth has been calculated to be 110 million curies, so that a few extra millicuries would not matter much. However, harmful *local* concentrations of isotope must be guarded against. Therefore, C^{14} can be discharged into sewers, but in amounts not greater than 1 millicurie per 100 gallons of liquid sewage. It can be converted to C^{14}-carbon dioxide gas by "cleaning solution" (a mixture of chromic and sulfuric acids), and discharged into the atmosphere at a rate not exceeding 100 microcuries per hour per sq. ft. of air intake area in the face of a hood.

4. SPILLS

In case of a spill, immediate confinement of the material is called for: if wet, by absorbent paper; if dry, by wetting it with water or oil. The material is then transferred to a container (the operator wears gloves), and the spot is decontaminated by washing (washings go into the radioactive waste container) or by treatment with "cleaning solution." Constant monitoring of the spill and the whole cleaning operation is imperative. Tracking of the spilled material by treading into it must be absolutely avoided.

Hands and clothing of the workers concerned must be constantly monitored during and at the end of the clean-up. Spills can be completely avoided, of course, by always working over trays and by keeping breakable vessels inside unbreakable (stainless steel) beakers.

Decontamination of C^{14}-labeled compounds is carried out by immersion of the material in "cleaning solution" for 24 hours in a fume hood. All C^{14} is converted to $C^{14}O_2$ in this way, and escapes up the hood. Decontamination is more difficult with H^3 and S^{35}, though the same cleaning solution is used, followed by thorough rinsing with running water. Other isotopes cannot be decontaminated in this way, and must be stored until the radioactivity has decayed, either in the workers' own laboratory or after returning it to Oak Ridge.

5. THE ISOTOPE LABORATORY

The construction of an isotope laboratory must take into account all the problems of radiation protection and decontamination discussed in the previous section. The floor should be covered with linoleum or asphalt tile which will not absorb radioactive liquids and can be easily removed and replaced. Work surfaces should be of stainless steel, or at least made of a smooth, nonporous material. Walls should be covered with enamel paint. There must be sufficient hood space provided for all radiochemical work over 40 microcuries in solution, or 1 microcurie in the solid state. The hoods should have stainless steel trays as bases and large sinks of the same material for decontamination. Air flow through the hoods should be high and constant (about 100 linear feet per minute) and, indeed, good ventilation of the whole laboratory is necessary for health. The hoods must have their own exhaust above the roof, high enough not to allow re-entry of the exhaust gases through windows.

High-level (energetic radiation emitters and high levels

of radioactivity) and low-level working areas should be separate. There must be a separate room which houses counting equipment. It should be kept free of all but mounted radioactive samples and be especially well guarded against contamination, in order to keep the background radioactivity of the counting instruments at a low level.

REFERENCES

National Bureau of Standards, U. S. (1952). Handbook Series 51: "Radiation Protection." Washington, D. C.

National Bureau of Standards, U. S. (1953). Handbook Series 52: "Maximum Permissible Dose of Radioisotopes." Washington, D. C.

Quimby, E. H., and Feitelberg, S. (1962). "Radioactive Isotopes in Medicine and Biology." Lea & Febiger, Philadelphia, Pennsylvania.

IV

Principles and Conditions for the Use of Isotopes in Biology

Section I. Identical Chemical and Biochemical Behavior of Isotopic Compounds

A. Cases of Nonidentical Chemical Behavior

1. THE ISOTOPE EFFECT

The tacit assumption is made by the isotope chemist that the isotopic compound behaves exactly like the normal compound. In fact, identical chemical behavior is the first condition for the use of isotopes in chemical or biological experiments. The aim is to trace the normal molecules through reactions and transformations. If the isotopic molecules are to be effective tracers, they must obviously behave in the same way as the normal ones. The radioactive molecule expresses its distinctiveness only at the moment of disintegration of the isotopic atom within it.

Chemical reactions between atoms depend on the number and arrangement of electrons orbiting around the nucleus, and these are identical for normal and isotopic atoms. However, the *rates* of chemical reactions are to some extent influenced by the mass of the reacting atoms, as well as by the number of electrons, and isotopes are, of course, different in mass from normal atoms. Therefore, differences

45

in behavior between isotopic and normal compounds will be observed, if one looks at reaction velocities and equilibria of reactions, or the consequences thereof. Molecules containing the lighter isotope react faster than those which carry the heavier one. This difference in behavior is called the Isotope Effect. It can generally be assumed to be negligible for the isotopes of carbon, since the differences between reaction rates depend on the ratio of the atomic weights, which for C^{12} and C^{14} is not far from unity (14/12). But it becomes a factor of some importance for the hydrogen isotopes, H^1, H^2, and H^3, since the ratio of atomic weights is now 2/1 or 3/1, and maximum rate differences can be 73% between H^3 and H^1.

Consider the decomposition of labeled urea by the enzyme urease. "Labeled urea" is normal urea, NH_2—$C^{12}O$—NH_2, with a small admixture of isotopic urea, NH_2—$C^{14}O$—NH_2. Urease, in the presence of water, transforms it to carbon dioxide and ammonia:

$$NH_2—CO—NH_2 + H_2O = CO_2 + 2NH_3$$

Since the C^{12} atoms of the normal urea react faster than the C^{14} atoms of the isotopic urea, the CO_2 at the beginning of the reaction will have more C^{12} than the original urea; in other words, its specific radioactivity (i.e., radioactivity per unit weight) will be lower. As the reaction proceeds, the C^{14} atoms of the isotopic urea catch up, and at 100% reaction the CO_2 has the same specific activity again as the original starting material, the urea. Therefore, if the reaction is stopped halfway, a difference in the chemical reactivity between the normal and isotopic urea shows up: more of the normal urea has been decomposed. If the reaction goes to completion, however, no isotope effect is observable. Nor are isotope effects found after equilibrium has been established in reversible reactions, since the isotope effect of the forward reaction is canceled by that of the backward reaction.

2. The Isotope Effect as a Nuisance

The isotope effect becomes a matter for serious concern in complex biological systems, where reactions do not usually go to completion, nor are equilibria established. This is especially true for rapidly growing systems, such as a small inoculum of algae growing in inorganic medium containing C^{14}-bicarbonate. Most of the reactions are in one direction (synthesis rather than breakdown), and products of one reaction, already enriched in the lighter isotope, are the starting materials for the next reaction, in which the lighter isotope again reacts preferably to the heavier. Thus a cumulation of the isotope effect results. In consequence, the specific radioactivity of the plant matter of the algae has been found to be as much as 24% below that of the inorganic bicarbonate of the medium. An isotope effect of this magnitude does not, of course, occur in cases where a "steady state" has been established. This means that an over-all equilibrium situation has been achieved, and synthetic reactions approximately balance degradative reactions. An amusing experiment to illustrate this point was performed by Buchanan and Nakao (1951) who set up a "microcosm," or miniature world, in an aquarium. The aquarium was completely sealed, contained algae, small plants, snails, small fish, and an inorganic medium with C^{14}-bicarbonate, and was irradiated by light to provide energy. The plants assimilated the CO_2 and supplied oxygen and food for the animals. The animals recirculated the CO_2 back to the plants. The aquarium was opened after 3 years, and the carbon of the plant and animal matter was analyzed: Table I shows the results. The isotope effects were quite small: only 2.8% for the plants grown here under steady state conditions, compared to 24% when grown rapidly. Curiously, for reasons not understood, a reverse isotope effect was observed (C^{14} taken up faster than C^{12}) in the inorganic carbon of the snail shells.

In the usual animal experiments with C^{14}, isotope effects approach the steady state condition, and are therefore considered to be negligible.

As was mentioned, the isotope effect is far from negligible when deuterium (H^2) or tritium (H^3) is used, since the

TABLE I

ISOTOPE EFFECT IN AQUARIUM[a]

	Specific activity %
CO_2 dissolved in water	100.0
Eel grass roots	95.3
Eel grass leaves	95.2
Duckweed	95.7
Snails	96.0
Snail shell carbonate	102.1

[a] From D. L. Buchanan and A. Nakao, *AEC Microcards* **AECU-1828** (1951).

rate differences here are huge. A quantitative interpretation of results obtained with compounds containing these isotopes, or with "doubly labeled" compounds (containing C^{14} as well as H^2), must take into account this difference in behavior.

3. THE ISOTOPE EFFECT AS A TOOL

As happens so often in science, a source of trouble and error which many researchers try hard to get rid of, can be turned right around and made into a useful tool for investigation. Thus, the isotope effect has recently been put to use in elucidating the mechanisms of enzymatic reactions. The experiments are so arranged that an isotope effect *will* occur—the opposite of the ordinary tracer experiment, in which isotope effects are avoided. For instance, it has been shown that the microorganism *Acetobacter suboxydans* oxidizes D-mannitol to D-fructose (Fig. 1). The three oxygen atoms, in positions 1, 2, and 3, have to be in

```
      CH₂OH  1                    CH₂OH  1
  HO—CH      2                    C=O    2
  HO—CH      3                HO—CH      3
   H—C—OH                      H—C—OH
   H—C—OH                      H—C—OH
      CH₂OH                       CH₂OH
   D-Mannitol                  D-Fructose


              CH₂OH  1
           H—C—OH    2
          HO—CH      3
           H—C—OH
           H—C—OH
              CH₂OH

            D-Sorbitol
```

Fig. 1. From Sniegoski *et al., Chem. Eng. News* **38** (Sept. 26), 58 (1960).

correct configuration for oxidation to take place; change one around, as in D-sorbitol, and the compound is simply not touched by the enzyme of the bacterium. From this, one can conclude that some kind of interaction or binding of these three atoms (1, 2, and 3) of the sugar to the enzyme takes place. The question then arises: is there a chemical reaction, involving valence bonds at these positions also? A study of the isotope effect gives a definite answer: if carbon 1 or 3 is labeled with C^{14}, the oxidation of the isotopic compounds goes on at the same rate as that of the normal. But if the carbon atom at position 2 is made isotopic (or the hydrogen attached to that carbon atom), then the rate is greatly slowed down. Conclusion: despite the steric specificity at carbons 1 and 3, no chemical reaction takes place there but only some form of loose binding to the enzyme. The enzymatic breaking of a chemical bond occurs exclusively at position 2.

The isotope effect can give the biochemist information

about the way a single carbon-hydrogen bond is broken
or formed in an enzymatic reaction which is part of a
"multi-enzyme" sequence in the intact animal. Take as an
example the conversion of glycerol to glycogen in the rat
(Rose, 1961). The reaction steps are outlined in Fig. 2. One

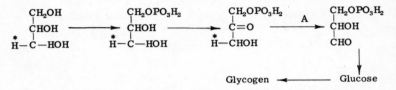

FIG. 2. Conversion of glycerol to glycogen in the rat. H*: replaced
by D (deuterium).

of the reaction steps (A), mediated by the enzyme triose
phosphate isomerase, requires the breaking of a C—H
bond. Consequently, when the H there is replaced by
deuterium, an isotope effect occurs, and the C—D bond
breaks more slowly than the C—H bond. Now, the question that interests the biochemist is: which is the rate-
determining (i.e., slowest) step in the whole sequence of
reactions (Fig. 2), when it happens in the intact animal?
This is answered by substituting a deuterium for a hydrogen
atom in the glycerol: we already know that a C—D bond
will react more slowly than a C—H bond. Then the reaction
sequence is compared in an animal receiving the C—H
glycerol to that receiving the C—D glycerol. Of course, not
all the glycerol reacts, so that one needs a marker for the
extent of the reaction. This is provided by labeling all the
glycerol (hydrogen- and deuterium-labeled) with C^{14} as
well, and determining the C^{14} in the resulting glycogen.
The comparison is then between the conversion of the
C^{14}-D and the C^{14}-H glycerol to glycogen (the C^{12}-C^{14}
isotope effect is negligible). If an isotope effect occurs,
that is, if the C^{14}-glycogen is formed more slowly from the
C^{14}-D than the C^{14}-H glycerol, then one knows that the
rate-determining step of the sequence is the breaking of

the C—H bond in the triose phosphate isomerase reaction. This was actually found to be the case. In this, as in many other more intricate ways, the isotope effect is finding an important place in isotope methodology.

B. Cases of Nonidentical Biological Behavior

4. RADIATION DAMAGE

Just as the mass difference between isotopic and normal atoms is the cause of differences in chemical behavior, so the characteristic property of radioisotopes, the emission of radiation, is the cause of differences in biological effect. Radiation causes ionization, and hence cell damage. Therefore, in experiments with radioisotopes used as tracers for normal atoms, the question always arises: how far can we neglect the damage to biological material brought about by the radiation, and not intended to be there?

It is obvious that the minimum dose of radioactive isotope which can be used with negligible tissue damage depends on the type, amount, and energy of radiation emitted. For instance, the National Bureau of Standards (1953) Handbook recommends for the rat no more than 11 microcuries of total-body retention of iron-59, an energetic β- and γ-emitter.

Beta-emitters are much less dangerous to tissue, since their radiation is readily absorbed by the aqueous medium surrounding the dissolved atoms. For instance, Heidelberger and Jones (1948) checked the danger of cancer induction by administration of labeled phosphorus (an energetic β-emitter), in the form of phosphate. Even as high a dose as 16 r per day per animal (mouse) caused no tumors. This is not to say, of course, that other, less obvious tissue damage might not have occurred and passed unnoticed.

For the weak β-emitters C^{14} and H^3 (tritium, T), the situation is even less serious. Almost no radiation penetrates the layer of water around the radiating atom beyond a few millimeters. However, there is one serious exception:

the effect on genetic material. This applies, of course, in a much greater degree to the more energetic isotopes, but they are used less in the labeling of genetic material than are C^{14} and T.

5. GENETIC DAMAGE BY RADIATION

Consider the following three cases: (*1*) A C^{14}-containing molecule is in solution in the aqueous medium of a cell; the β-radiation which it emits is instantly absorbed and inactivated by the water molecules around it. (*2*) A C^{14}-containing amino acid is part of a protein molecule; the radiation may either be absorbed by the aqueous solvent, or it may hit a neighbor in the chain of amino acids that makes up the protein molecule. In the latter case, a chemical change would occur in the protein molecule, and its enzymatic activity may decrease or be abolished altogether. Since the number of isotopic amino acids in a single protein molecule would be small, and since only a very few protein molecules in an ordinary labeling experiment would carry labeled amino acids anyway, the consequences to the cell and its metabolism would be completely unnoticeable. A minute fraction of the total amount of a particular enzyme destroyed means nothing to the cell: it will be immediately replaced by the protein turnover machinery. (*3*) A C^{14}-containing nucleotide is part of a deoxyribonucleic acid (DNA) molecule. This is the genetic material of the cell. Every enzyme synthesized, and therefore everything the cell makes and does, is completely dependent on the chemical structure of the gene or, in chemical terms, the DNA molecules. Change that structure, and the wrong protein will be made, not just once but over and over again. The consequences of being supplied with an enzyme which cannot do its job, or does it wrongly, and of not having this error corrected immediately but, on the contrary, causing it to be inherited by other cells, are catastrophic to the organism. This is inherent in the concept of the unique

chemical structure of every DNA molecule and its exact replication in the reproduction of the cell.

The β-rays emitted by the labeled nucleotide may be absorbed and rendered harmless by the surrounding water molecules; or they may hit another nucleotide of the DNA chain and thereby bring about a chemical change within the molecule and hence a genetic change. Genetic damage caused in this way has been observed more often with tritium than C^{14}, although the β-radiation of T is much weaker than that of C^{14}. The reason for this is that much higher specific activities can be obtained with T (as explained in Chap. I. Sect. 8). The fact that the range of the low-energy radiation of T is short does not really hinder the process, since only molecular distances are involved (from one nucleotide to the next).

The nucleotide which is incorporated specifically into DNA is thymidine. In plants (onion root tips) grown with C^{14}-thymidine, as much as 20% of the cells were found to have aberrations due to chromosome breaks. In tissue culture, 90% of cells have been found to die when the culture was grown in 0.1 microcurie of T-labeled thymidine. In a mouse, as little as 5 microcuries of T-thymidine per gram resulted in sperm cell lesions.

In general, it is assumed that 50 r (roentgens) per kg. gives rise to genetic damage. Table II illustrates the relation of dose to radiation effect expressed in roentgens.

It is interesting to note how, once again, as in the case of the isotope effect, a disadvantage and a nuisance is not eliminated, but deliberately applied as a new tool for research. This was done with the radiation effect of radioactive isotopes on biological systems. Hershey and his associates (1951) found that viruses which take up radioactive phosphorus (P^{32}) are killed by the isotope. Between specific activities of 10 and 100 millicuries per mg. of phosphorus (30–300 atoms of P^{32} per total P), the rate of death of viruses is a measure of the specific radioactivity

of the virus. An assay of the P^{32} taken up by the virus can
thus be obtained. It is derived from the straight-line relationship between the log of surviving viruses against time,
with the slope depending on the amount of P^{32} taken up.
The authors established the important fact that, in their
system at least (P^{32} in viruses), it is not the ionization

TABLE II
Dose of Isotope Giving a Radiation Equivalent to
(a) 0.1 r for 24 Hours after Administration or (b) 0.3 r/Week[a],[b]

Isotope	Dose (μc./kg.)	
	a	b
Tritium (H^3)	—	140
Carbon (C^{14})	32	3
Phosphorus (P^{32})	2.4	0.14
Sulfur (S^{35})	30	4.3
Iodine (I^{131})	8.3	0.08

[a] From H. R. V. Arnstein and P. T. Grant, *Progr. in Biophys.* **7**,
185 (1957).

[b] Data for (a) calculated by Marinelli *et al.* (1948), assuming uniform
distribution of isotope; those for (b) given in the report of the Inter-
national Commission on Radiological Protection (1954), assuming non-
uniform distribution.

brought about by the β-radiation that is the cause of death
of the cells, but the actual nuclear reaction ($P^{32} \rightarrow S^{32}$, the
disintegration of the radioactive phosphorus atom to the
stable sulfur atom; see Chap. I, Sect. 5). Presumably the
chemical change in a DNA molecule from phosphorus to
sulfur was enough to inactivate the molecule's functions.
About 12 disintegrations per virus were enough to kill it.

6. The Dosage Problem

How much of a labeled compound should be injected or
fed to an animal? How much should be added to a cell
suspension or cell homogenate? Two factors have to be

considered: the radioactivity and the weight of the dose.

The main reason for avoiding an excessively high dose of radioactivity has been outlined in this chapter (Sect. I-B-4). Another reason is simply that of economy: isotopic compounds are expensive. Besides, consideration of the health of the investigator precludes use of excessively high doses. On the other hand, a sufficiently high dose of radioactivity must be given so that, after dilution with nonradioactive material within the animal or other biological system, and all the vagaries of extraction, the sample assayed will have a measurably large amount of radioactivity. The weight of radioactive compound should, of course, be small. In the days when isotopic compounds were not available, metabolic studies were sometimes done by *overdosing* an animal with the compound under study, and then looking for unusual excretion products in the urine. Today it is possible to investigate metabolic pathways, with infinitely greater precision and in enormous detail, with a *physiological dose* of the compound in isotopic form. The daily intake by the rat of the amino acid histidine, for instance, is about 80 mg. In any study of the metabolism of histidine in the normal animal, it would obviously be very undesirable to feed more than that per day. Labeled histidine is commercially available with a specific activity of 1 millicurie per millimole (155 mg.). Consider a dose of radioactivity for a 120-gm. rat. It must be neither so high as to cause radiation damage, nor so low as to lead to immeasurably small radioactivity in the final product to be isolated. This dose would be 0.1–0.2 millicurie, or 15–30 mg., an amount that could be easily fed in two or three meals without upsetting the normal feeding pattern of the animal. However, not always can we be so lucky as to have available compounds with so high a specific activity. It usually happens that specific activities are too low. The investigator will then often yield to the temptation of administering as much radioactivity as he needs, irrespective of the weight given. Suppose the labeled histidine he can get has only 0.01 millicurie per millimole; he might then feed 10 millimoles (1.55 gm.) of histidine to the animal—a gross overdose—to attain the desired radioactivity of 0.1 millicurie. The pitfalls of over-dosing with material of low specific activity were well illustrated by an example given by Arnstein and Grant (1957). They found that, with an experimental diet often used containing 2% of α-labeled glycine, the β-carbon atom of serine becomes labeled (as shown below) to the extent of 36% of the total radioactivity in the serine, a considerable extent of

$$\overset{\alpha}{C}H_2(NH_2)COOH \rightarrow HO\overset{\beta}{C}H_2CH(NH_2)COOH$$
$$\text{Glycine} \qquad\qquad\qquad \text{Serine}$$

conversion. On a 0.5% glycine diet the serine β-carbon gets only 20%, and on a normal rat diet containing 0.1% glycine only 15% of the label. The erroneous conclusion from the first experiment would be that the normal pathway of the α-carbon of glycine is transformation into the β-carbon of serine. In fact, this is true only for an overdose of glycine.

7. Factors Influencing Dosage

Why was 0.1 millicurie chosen as a reasonable dose of radioactivity for a rat? What is the basis for dosage calculation? The given fact in calculating dosage is the radioactivity necessary for assay in the final sample isolated. This must be sufficiently high so that, with the ordinary counting equipment available, an assay of reasonable accuracy can be made. Simple statistics will tell how long a sample must be counted for a given degree of accuracy. A discussion of counting statistics is out of place here and will be treated separately in another book of this series. However, one can see intuitively, that with a background count of, say, 20 counts per minute (caused by cosmic radiation and other stray "noise" not due to the sample) and a sample count of, say, 3 c.p.m., one would have to take background and background-plus-sample measurements many, many times over to get a reasonable degree of certainty; for the background activity might fluctuate like this: 19 c.p.m.; 18 c.p.m.; 23 c.p.m.; 20 c.p.m., etc.; and the background-plus-sample counts might read: 22 c.p.m.; 25 c.p.m.; 23 c.p.m.; 20 c.p.m., etc.

Therefore, in dosage calculations it is usually the aim for the final sample isolated to have a radioactivity 5–10 times that of the background.

The factors to be considered in a whole-animal experiment that would influence the amount of dose to be given are the following:

(1) Feeding *versus* injection; feeding, of course, is the normal, physiological way, but a large fraction of the compound may be lost because of incomplete absorption.

(2) How many intermediate steps are there between the administered compound and the final product to be isolated and assayed? What is the rate of metabolism of these intermediates? To what extent are they changed into compounds other than the desired product?

(3) How far is the compound, or the intermediates derived from it, excreted or transported into inaccessible tissues or storage sites? How much of it will be widely distributed in a variety of tissues?

(4) What dilution with nonradioactive material already existing in the organism can be expected of the injected compound, of the intermediates, and of the final product?

(5) What is the duration of the experiment? Should the dose be given once, or divided into portions and given several times, or infused continuously?

It is obvious that little firm information would exist about any of the above points in the planning of an experiment. Indeed, the isotope experiment is often performed precisely for the purpose of gaining this type of information. Nonetheless, decisions must be made as to the dosages to be used.

One thing can be predicted with certainty: in an *in vitro* experiment, with a cell suspension or homogenate or an enzyme solution, vastly less isotope is needed because of the simplicity of the system; there are far fewer intermediates and side reactions, far less dilution with nonradioactive material, and no excretion.

If 100 microcuries (0.1 millicurie) is a reasonable dose for a 100-gm. rat, 1–2 μc. might be enough for a homogenate from a gram of rat liver. This is merely a coarse rule-of-thumb, and every proper isotope experiment ought to be preceded by a pilot or orientation experiment, to determine the correct dose level.

Section II. Constant Natural Abundance

The first basic assumption of the isotope experimenter, that of identical behavior of isotopic and normal compounds, has been discussed. Another is that of constant natural abundance. Many of the isotopes used in biology occur naturally, deuterium (H^2), for instance, to the extent of 0.2% of total hydrogen. Supposing that in an experiment one wished to measure exceedingly low concentrations of deuterium (of the order of 0.2%); one would have to be certain that at all times and in all places the naturally occurring deuterium would not rise above or fall below the 0.2%, or else the error in the measurement of the artificially added isotope would be large. This condition—constant natural abundance—generally holds in practice. There is, however, one important exception: radioactive carbon (C^{14}).

1. RADIOCARBON DATING

Naturally occurring C^{14} decays continuously, though at a very slow rate: given any amount of it, one half of that amount will disappear by decay in about 5,000 years. But it is also continuously replenished by the neutrons of cosmic radiation bombarding the nitrogen of the upper atmosphere. A nuclear reaction takes place, with which we are familiar from the atomic reactor (see Chap. I, Sect. 5):

$$_7N^{14} + _0n^1 \rightarrow _6C^{14} + _1H^1$$

The new C^{14} enters the atmosphere as $C^{14}O_2$, becomes absorbed by plants, and is built into their substance. The plants are eaten by animals, which then expire the C^{14} as CO_2. The isotope thus participates in the world's carbon cycle. This, then, is how the loss by decay of the world's radioactive carbon is replenished. But not *all* the world's carbon, because not all of it participates in the carbon cycle: that carbon which is not in exchange with atmospheric CO_2 cannot get a share of the replenishment by the $C^{14}O_2$ newly formed by cosmic ray bombardment. This is the carbon trapped in coal, petroleum, or chalk deposits; the carbon in wood preserved underground, or in sealed-off places; the carbon in the mummies inside pyramids—it all continues to decay, of course, at the rate characteristic for C^{14}. The consequence is that "fossil" carbon has less radioactivity than carbon from fresh plants or animals. Knowing the decay curve for C^{14}, it is possible to calculate the length of time the C^{14} of the particular specimen has been disintegrating without replenishment, for how many years it has been outside the carbon cycle, buried or removed from exchange with atmospheric CO_2; in other words, how old it is. This is the basis for the method of radiocarbon dating, discovered by Libby (1955). The difficulty of the method lies in the fact that the radioactivity of naturally occurring (i.e., replenished) C^{14} is very low (13.5 disintegrations per minute per gm. of carbon, for contemporary carbon), and that of old carbon, of course, even lower (6.75 d.p.m. per gm. of C after $5,568 \pm 30$ years). In consequence, for accurate measurement, large samples of carbon are needed, and background must be drastically reduced. To prepare and count large samples, with high carbon concentration, requires special sample preparation tech-

TABLE III

Age Determinations on Samples of Known Age[a]

Sample	Specific activity (c.p.m./gm. of carbon)		Age (years)	
	Found	Expected	Found	Expected
Tree ring (excavated Douglas fir)	11.10 ± 0.31 11.52 ± 0.35 11.34 ± 0.25 10.15 ± 0.44 11.08 ± 0.31 Average: 10.99 ± 0.15	10.65	1100 ± 150	1372 ± 50 (577 ± 50 A.D.)
Ptolemy (wood from mummy coffin)	9.5 ± 0.45	9.67	2300 ± 450	2149 ± 150 (200 ± 150 B.C.)
Tayinat (wood from Hittite palace)	8.97 ± 0.31 9.03 ± 0.30 9.53 ± 0.32 Average: 9.18 ± 0.18	9.10	2600 ± 150	2624 ± 50 (675 ± 50 B.C.)
Redwood	8.81 ± 0.26 8.56 ± 0.22 Average: 8.68 ± 0.17	8.78	3005 ± 165	2928 ± 52 (979 ± 52 B.C.)

Sesostris III (wood from funerary boat)	7.73 ± 0.36	7.90	3700 ± 400	3792 ± 50
	8.21 ± 0.50			(1843 ± 50 B.C.)
	Average:			
	7.97 ± 0.30			
Zoser: Sneferu (wood from Egyptian tombs)		7.15	4750 ± 250	
Zoser	7.88 ± 0.74			4650 ± 75
	7.36 ± 0.53			(2700 ± 75 B.C.)
Sneferu	6.95 ± 0.40			4575 ± 75
	7.42 ± 0.38			(2625 ± 75 B.C.)
	6.26 ± 0.41			Average:
	Average:			4600 ± 75
	7.04 ± 0.20			(2650 ± 75 B.C.)

[a] From J. R. Arnold and W. F. Libby, *Science* **110**, 678 (1949).

niques, too complex to be described here. The counting equipment is elaborate and made of special materials, since background radioactivity must be lowered from the usual 15–20 to 2–3 c.p.m. (Background counts are caused not only by cosmic radiation, but also by the natural radioactivity innate in the material of which counters are constructed.)

The method of radiocarbon dating has become phenomenally successful. As shown in Table III, it checks well with ages of carbon specimens determined by archeologists through other, independent methods. It is now a matter of routine to cross-check archeological dates by radiocarbon dating.

An ingenious sideline of radiocarbon dating has been the detection of river water pollution. Since petroleum and coal have been buried for so long that practically all their radioactivity has decayed, the natural radioactivity of these materials is practically zero. Now, the vast majority of industrial chemical products is made from petroleum or coal. If the carbonaceous matter from a sample of river water is collected, converted to carbon, and its natural radioactivity measured, it will be anywhere between zero and 13.5 d.p.m. per gm. of C. If the figure is 13.5, no pollution has taken place, since all the carbon is contemporary (i.e., living). If the figure is zero, all the carbon would be from chemical pollution. If it is between these two extremes, the extent of pollution can be calculated.

Section III. Chemical Stability of Isotopic Compounds

A condition sometimes overlooked by the isotope biologist is that "the isotope must stick." In using any ionic isotopic compound such as $Na^{24}Cl$, it will be obvious to any investigator that the labeled Na^{24} ion can exchange freely with unlabeled Na^{23} ions in solution. Even in an insoluble precipitate suspended in a solution, for instance $BaS^{35}O_4$, the labeled ions ($S^{35}O_4^{--}$) in the precipitate exchange freely with unlabeled ions ($S^{32}O_4^{--}$) in solution. In other words, an insoluble precipitate of a labeled salt suspended in a solution of unlabeled salt will rapidly lose its radioactivity to the solution, whereas the unlabeled material from the solution will enter the solid, until an equilibrium is established. Solid barium C^{14}-carbonate or sodium C^{14}-bicarbonate, when left in contact with moist air and CO_2, rapidly loses its C^{14}—again, not by a weight loss, but by an exchange with the nonradioactive CO_2 of the atmosphere.

1. CALCIUM ABSORPTION; THE INTESTINAL LOOP

Investigators sometimes utilize the easy exchange of labeled with unlabeled ions precisely for the purpose of studying this exchange. Harrison and Harrison (1960) investigated the function of vitamin D in the absorption of calcium ions from the intestine. They invented an ingenious technique for the purpose: the inverted intestinal loop. A piece of rat intestine is turned inside out, like a glove. The *outside* of the resulting tube is now the part that once formed the intestinal wall facing the gut (mucosal side); the *inside* of the tube is now that part which normally is in contact with the blood circulation (serosal side). It is thus an excellent tool for the study of intestinal absorption because, when this tube is shaped into a loop and suspended in a solution representing the intestinal contents, the transfer of material from this solution into the inside of the tube is an *in vitro* model of the transfer of substances from the gut into the bloodstream. In the present experiment, calcium ions were added to the solution outside ("intestinal contents"), and an artificial blood serum also containing calcium ions was placed inside the tube. When radioactive calcium chloride ($Ca^{45}Cl_2$) was now put into the outside solution, the radioactivity rapidly diffused into the tube (through the intestinal wall, into the "blood serum"). When using loops from vitamin D-deficient animals, the diffusion of Ca^{45} ions was half that found with normal intestine. The authors neatly demonstrated that this was diffusion and not active (enzymatic) transport, since the rate of transfer of labeled Ca ions from the mucosal to the serosal side was unaffected by a drop in temperature, and by respiration inhibitors. Moreover, the decrease with time of radioactivity on the mucosal side was exponential, as it would be in a diffusion process. It was concluded that vitamin D so affects the intestinal wall as to make possible the efficient diffusion of calcium ions through it.

There is one element, hydrogen, which can cause trouble by unsuspected exchange reactions in biochemical experiments. The oxygen-hydrogen bond is easily broken by ionization. Consider the enzymatic conversion of malic acid to citric acid:

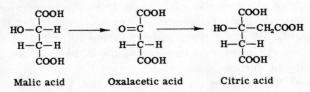

Malic acid   Oxalacetic acid   Citric acid

If a tritium atom replaces the hydrogen in malic acid, as shown, it would not reappear in the citric acid, but get lost by ionization in oxalacetic acid, the intermediate compound between malic and citric acids:

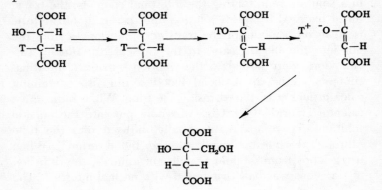

If one were ignorant of the occurrence of oxalacetic acid as an intermediate, one would be hard put to it to explain the loss of tritium from malic acid in its transformation to citric acid.

REFERENCES

Arnstein, H. R. V., and Grant, P. T. (1957). *Progr. in Biophys.* **7,** 184.

Buchanan, D. L., and Nakao, A. (1951). *AEC Microcards* **AECU-1828.**

Harrison, H. E., and Harrison, H. C. (1960). *Am. J. Physiol.* **199,** 265.

Heidelberger, C., and Jones, H. B. (1948). *Cancer* **1,** 252.

Hershey, A. D., Kamen, M. D., Kennedy, J. W., and Gest, H. (1951). *J. Gen. Physiol.* **34,** 305.

Libby, W. F. (1955). "Radiocarbon Dating." Univ. of Chicago Press, Chicago, Illinois.

National Bureau of Standards, U. S. (1953). Handbook Series 52. "Maximum Permissible Dose of Radioisotopes." Washington, D. C.

Rose, I. A. (1961). *J. Biol. Chem.* **236,** 603.

Sniegoski, L. T., Frush, H. L., and Isbell, H. S. (1960). *Chem. Eng. News* **38** (Sept. 26) 58.

V

Methods

Section I. The Isotope Dilution Method

The isotope dilution method, or carrier or trapping technique, as it has been called in its many adaptations, lies at the heart of isotope methodology. It is used mainly in three ways:

(a) in the isolation, purification, and identification of unknown intermediates in a chain of metabolic reactions;

(b) to obtain evidence of synthesis (incorporation), and precursor-product relationships between known compounds;

(c) as an analytical tool in the assay of known compounds.

A. The Isotope Dilution Method in the Isolation, Purification, and Characterization of Unknown Compounds

1. CRYSTALLIZATION TO CONSTANT SPECIFIC ACTIVITY

An example from the classical work of Calvin and his team on the fixation of carbon dioxide in the process of photosynthesis illustrates well this type of isotope dilution (Calvin and Bassham, 1957, 1962). A suspension of algae, in presence of labeled CO_2, was irradiated with light to cause photosynthesis to take place. This light exposure lasted for very short periods only. Within a matter of a second or so, a single labeled compound was detectable in an extract of the plants. This compound evidently was the first to become labeled. What was this substance? It was available in minute amounts only, of course, but highly radioactive. The substance was purified by paper chromatography (see Chap. V, Sect. II-1), a technique for which radioactivity alone rather than quantity is sufficient as an indicator of behavior. It was found that the compound was acidic, contained a phosphate group, and might be related to a phosphorylated 3-carbon sugar. Next came a crucial step: an educated guess of what the compound might be. The guess was "educated," because the researchers had learnt something about the properties of the compound from its behavior on chromatography; also because their knowledge of biochemistry was sufficiently wide to allow them to predict with a certain degree of confidence what type of compound one might expect in the first stages of photosynthesis.

Their guess was: phosphoglyceric acid (PGA). This material was obtained in good amounts by extraction from green plants or algae, in nonradioactive form of course. A small quantity of it was mixed in solution with the practically weightless radioactive unknown, in the form of the barium salt, and repeatedly crystallized. Suppose the nonradioactive PGA weighed 5 mg. and the total "weightless" radioactive compound had 10,000 c.p.m. Then the specific activity of the mixture would be 10,000/5 or 2,000 c.p.m. per mg. Suppose, first, that the radioactive unknown compound were different from PGA. Then, upon the first crystallization, the radioactive material would not become mixed with the crystals of PGA as they settled out of solution, since only identical molecules adhere to each other in crystal formation. In consequence, the crystals obtained in the first crystallization would be nonradioactive, or at least would have a specific activity much lower than 2,000 c.p.m. per mg. Certainly, further crystallizations would lead to zero radioactivity in the PGA.

On the other hand, if the unknown radioactive compound were identical with the nonradioactive PGA, then, upon the first crystallization, since in solution all molecules (radioactive and nonradioactive) are homogeneously mixed and all identical, the crystals formed would be radioactive. What is more, their specific activity would be 2,000 c.p.m. per mg., because 5 mg. of nonradioactive PGA was mixed with 10,000 c.p.m. of "weightless" radioactive PGA. The beauty of the procedure lies in the fact that not all of the 5 mg. of PGA need be recovered in the crystallization, to make this observation. Far from it; one can determine the specific activity with, say, 0.5 mg. (1,000 c.p.m.). Of course, one crystallization is not enough, the material must be crystallized many times, preferably from different solvents, to *constant specific activity*. Then the identity of the unknown radioactive compound and the "carrier" PGA is assured, or at least made very probable. Other criteria, of course, have to be applied.

2. IDENTIFICATION OF METABOLITES

The method is well illustrated by an experiment performed for the identification of a metabolite of the cancer-producing compound (carcinogen) dibenzanthracene (Heidelberger and Wiest, 1951). This substance has the property of causing the growth of tumors if applied to the skin of mice. Naturally it is of importance to find out what happens to the compound in the animal, in order to get clues to the mechanism of transformation of the normal to the cancerous cell. In short, what is the metabolism of the carcinogen? Its structure is shown in Fig. 1. In this figure, the presence of the two OH groups denotes the structure of a known metabolite of the carcinogen. The asterisks show the position of radioactivity. When the labeled car-

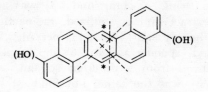

FIG. 1. (Dihydroxy) dibenzanthracene.

cinogen was administered to mice, radioactivity appeared in the feces. The weight of this radioactive fecal metabolite was, of course, much too small to permit isolation or identification by classical chemical procedures. However, merely by exploration of the properties of the *weightless* radioactive substance, some information of its character was gained: it was acidic, and the label was located in its acid groups ($C^{14}OOH$), attached to a ring (they were lost as $C^{14}O_2$ on heating). The stage was set for the judicious guess: an acid derived from the already known metabolite could be formed by oxidative breakdown along any of the three dashed lines shown in Fig. 1. The resulting three acids are shown in Fig. 2.

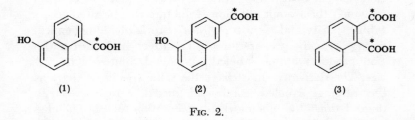

FIG. 2.

Each one of the three was prepared synthetically in non-radioactive form, of course, and in gram quantities, and crystallized with the weightless radioactive material from the feces extract. Compounds (1) and (2) lost all radio-activity after the first crystallization. Therefore, neither could be identical with the radioactive metabolite from feces. When 10 mg. of compound (3) was added to the radioactive extract and crystallized, radioactivity was recovered in the crystals—75 c.p.m. per mg. The crystals were sublimed: specific activity, 68 c.p.m. per mg. They were crystallized from a different solvent, and still the specific activity was the same. For final establishment of the identity of the synthetic, nonradioactive, and the metabolic, radioactive compound, they were both dissolved in ether. The ether solution was shaken with aqueous acetic acid. Compound (3) as well as the radioactivity distributed themselves between the two solvents. The distribution coefficients, K, were:

$$K = \frac{\text{mg. in ether}}{\text{mg. in acetic acid}} = 4.2; \qquad K^* = \frac{\text{c.p.m. in ether}}{\text{c.p.m. in acetic acid}} = 4.5$$

It is obvious, from the close similarity of the distribution of weight of "carrier" and weightless radioactive metabolite, that the two must be identical.

3. RADIOCHEMICAL PURITY

The three methods discussed—crystallization, sublimation, solvent distribution—are only a few examples of ways in which the isotope dilution technique can be used to establish purity and identity. Other "criteria of radiochemical purity" are: the preparation of derivatives, and of degradation products of the labeled compound diluted with carrier. The derivative must have the same specific activity as the original labeled compound mixed with carrier. In degradation—the chemical fragmentation of the labeled compound together with the carrier—the sum of the isotope content of the fragments must add up to that of the whole compound before degradation. Always, the mass dilution must be the same as the dilution in radioactivity. As put by Arnstein and Grant (1957), "The only satisfactory criterion of purity for labeled compounds is the complete association of the isotope with the compound in question."

4. CHROMATOGRAPHY; "COINCIDENCE OF PEAKS"

A useful variation on this theme is the application of chromatography to isotope dilution—chromatography in one of its many variants: absorption, partition, ion-exchange, gas, paper, or thin-layer chromatography. The principle is the same. The labeled compound is mixed with unlabeled carrier. The mixture is placed on the chromatographic column. Solvent is washed through the column, and fractions of equal volume are collected in a series of tubes. The carrier compound, together with the labeled compound, will move down the column. If they are identical, they will have the same properties in relation to the absorbent or ion-exchange resin in the column. They will, therefore, move down the column at the same rate and emerge in the same fraction. Two curves can be plotted: volume of solvent eluted or fraction number against weight, and against radioactivity. If the curves coincide ("coincidence of peaks"), then the carrier compound and the radioactive compound are identical (Fig. 3). For every point representing a fraction number, radioactivity divided by weight must be the same (i.e., specific activity is constant). Shown on the graph in Fig. 3 are also peaks of radioactivity unaccompanied by measurable weight; these are meant to show radioactive impurities which are separated on the column. Instead of direct weight, such other measurements of quantity as light absorption in the ultraviolet region or colorimetric assay can be substituted.

A particularly elegant application of the method of coincidence of peaks is the combination of gas chromatography and liquid scintillation counting. If a mixture of liquid substances, such as for instance the esters of fatty acids, is volatilized by raising the temperature, and the vapor flushed by a stream of helium gas through a long column packed with absorbent and kept at the elevated temperature, then each compound in the mixture—each ester, say

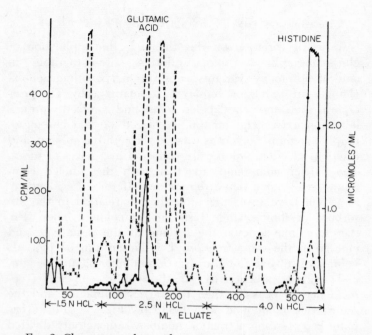

FIG. 3. Chromatographic analysis on an ion exchange resin column of the nonprotein fraction of rabbit liver 40 minutes after injection of radioactive histidine. The radioactivity of the eluate fractions, expressed as counts per minute per milliliter, is shown by solid lines. The weight of amino acids in the same eluate fractions, expressed as μmoles per milliliter is shown by dash lines. In this experiment, the amino acids which are naturally present in rabbit liver act as "carrier"; it can be seen that the two labeled compounds present are glutamic acid and histidine, since the radioactivity-peaks coincide with the known weight peaks for these two amino acids (Abrams and Borsook, 1952).

—will travel through the column at a different rate and emerge at a different time after the injection of the mixture into the column. Very sensitive means have been devised for detection and quantitation of the emerging vapor fractions. If the exit from the column dips straight into a vial of solvent for the liquid scintillation counter (see Chap. I, Sect. 6), then the compound dissolves as it comes off the column and can be counted. Thus in one operation, which can be automated, one obtains: (*a*) separation of a mixture into separate constituents, shown as peaks on a chart; (*b*) estimation of the weight of compound in each peak; (*c*) assay of radioactivity in each peak. The specific activity of each constituent of the mixture can then be calculated. Carrier compounds can be put through the column with the mixture, and coincidence of peaks will reveal identity of carrier and unknown. The beauty of the method lies in the tremendous resolving power of the column, the speed and ease of operation, and the sensitivity of the detecting system.

5. CHEMICAL STRUCTURE ESTABLISHED BY RADIOCHEMICAL MEANS

A brilliant example of the carrier method can be found in the work of Bloch and his collaborators (Gautschi and Bloch 1957, 1958). Cholesterol is synthesized by the liver of animals. One of its precursors is lanosterol. Bloch found, however, that lanosterol is not converted directly to cholesterol; another compound (called X) makes its fleeting and transient appearance. Slices of rat liver, when suspended in a medium resembling blood serum to which a trace of highly radioactive sodium acetate has been added, convert the acetate to labeled lanosterol and cholesterol. However, before cholesterol appeared, the intermediate X was detected in the mixture. It disappeared again as it was being transformed into cholesterol. It must, therefore, be an intermediate between lanosterol and cholesterol. This intermediate was never found in quantities that could be seen or weighed. It was only detected as radioactivity, eluted from a chromatography column in a different fraction than either lanosterol or cholesterol. It was not possible to guess its structure, synthesize it, and then use it as carrier in identification experiments. Instead, its immediate precursor, lanosterol, was used as carrier (this compound is available in quantity) and, *with the full knowledge* that X differed from lanosterol (though only slightly), a series of chemical reactions was carried out with the mixture of unlabeled carrier lanosterol and radioactive, weightless X. These reactions revealed the similarities *and differences* between lanosterol and X. In this way, though X has never been seen by anyone, its chemical structure was completely established.

B. Isotope Dilution as a Means for Studying the Synthesis of Known Compounds

6. ISOTOPE TRAPPING

This method is the same as method (*a*), except that the labeled intermediate, which is being diluted by unlabeled carrier, is a known compound. The investigator wants to find out if, in reaction $A \rightarrow C$, compound B is an intermediate. He runs the reaction with labeled A and obtains labeled C. When the reaction is complete, he adds unlabeled carrier B. If B occurs as an intermediate in the reaction, the carrier B molecules will mix with the labeled B molecules and thus pick up the label:

$$A^* \rightarrow B^* \rightarrow C^*$$
$$\uparrow$$
$$B$$

The unlabeled carrier need not be added after the reaction is complete, but may be present while it is actually going on. This is called "isotope trapping." For instance, a homogenate of rat liver was incubated with radioactive histidine and unlabeled carrier urocanic acid. At the end of the incubation period, both histidine and urocanic acid were isolated and purified to constant specific activity. Table I shows the results. At the start of the incubation, histidine had all the radioactivity, urocanic acid none. At the end, histidine had less and urocanic acid was labeled. Yet in the absence of carrier urocanic acid, this substance would not have accumulated and could not have been detected as an intermediate in the breakdown of histidine. The method

TABLE I

TRAPPING OF 2-C^{14}-LABELED HISTIDINE IN UROCANIC ACID BY GUINEA PIG LIVER HOMOGENATES[a,b]

Compound	μmole	c.p.m. per μmole	Total c.p.m.
Initial L-Histidine	29	10,750	312,000
Initial urocanic acid	762	—	—
Final L-histidine	14.2[c]	10,750[c]	153,000
Final urocanic acid	593	195	116,000[d]

[a] From A. H. Mehler and H. Tabor, *J. Biol. Chem.* **201**, 775 (1953).

[b] 20 ml. of uncentrifuged guinea pig liver homogenate (representing 4 gm. of liver) were incubated at 37° with labeled histidine and unlabeled urocanic acid in a total volume of 42 ml. at pH 8. At zero time and after 5.5 hours, a 20-ml. aliquot was mixed with 200 μM of unlabeled histidine acidified with 1 ml. of 1 N acetic acid, and boiled for 1 minute. Histidine and urocanic acid were then isolated as previously described.

[c] Calculated.

[d] This figure represents a minimal value for the conversion of histidine to urocanic acid, since some of the labeled urocanic acid formed was further metabolized during the experiment. If it is assumed that the specific activity of the urocanic acid metabolized is the average of the initial and final specific activities, an additional 18,000 c.p.m. should be added to the amount found in urocanic acid. This calculation assumes a constant activity of histidase and urocanase during the course of the experiment. In a separate experiment this has been shown to be true for urocanase. However, since histidase is not saturated with histidine, even at the beginning of the experiment, the rate of formation of urocanic acid decreases with time. Since we cannot evaluate this change precisely, the 18,000 c.p.m. is a minimal value. Therefore, at least $(116,000 + 18,000)/159,000 \times 100$ or 84% of the histidine degraded was converted to urocanic acid.

can be taken a step further, and the carrier administered to a whole animal together with the labeled compound. When C^{14}-glycine was given to a rat together with a large dose of unlabeled carrier formic acid (as sodium formate), the formic acid excreted in the urine of the rat within a few hours was radioactive, showing that glycine is metabolized to formic acid to some extent.

7. REVERSE ISOTOPE TRAPPING

This method can be varied almost indefinitely. For instance: instead of adding unlabeled carrier to dilute the isotopic compound in the biological system, one can administer the labeled compound and follow its dilution by the unlabeled species *made by the living organism*. A good example of this technique is the following (Newman and Zilversmit, 1962). The problem was the origin of cholesterol formed in the aorta of rabbits suffering from atherosclerosis: is it deposited from the plasma, or is it synthesized by the tissue within the walls of the aorta? To answer this question, C^{14}-cholesterol was fed to rabbits to the extent of 1% in the diet. Plasma and aorta cholesterol were isolated, and their specific activity was determined. If the aorta cholesterol were synthesized by the tissue in the walls of the aorta, it would, of course, be unlabeled and its specific radioactivity would be zero. If some labeled cholesterol were deposited from the plasma in the aorta, the unlabeled cholesterol synthesized in the aorta would dilute the isotopic plasma cholesterol derived from the diet. The specific activity of the aorta cholesterol would always be lower than that of the plasma cholesterol. If, on the other hand, aorta cholesterol were derived entirely by deposition of plasma cholesterol in the walls of the aorta, pre-existing unlabeled aorta cholesterol would gradually be replaced by plasma cholesterol, until the two reached the same specific activity level. A clear-cut answer was obtained in the experiment: Table II shows that, with prolonged feeding of cholesterol, the specific activity of aorta cholesterol started low and increased until it reached the same value as plasma cholesterol. The latter, therefore, is the source of the cholesterol found in the aorta.

TABLE II

INTIMA AND PLASMA CHOLESTEROL SPECIFIC ACTIVITIES[a]

Animal no.	Days on 1% C^{14}-cholesterol diet	Free cholesterol specific activity	
		Intima[b] (c.p.m./mg.)	Intima/terminal plasma
1	21	133	0.394
2	21	388	0.828
3	21	226	0.492
4	21	300	0.595
5	25	373	0.825
6	30	401	1.19
7	43	356	1.02
8	87	409	1.00

[a] From H. A. I. Newman and D. B. Zilversmit, *J. Biol. Chem.* **237,** 2078 (1962).

[b] Intima derived from the whole thoracic aorta. Intima denotes the inner lining of the aorta, in contact with the blood.

C. Isotope Dilution as an Analytical Tool

8. ISOTOPE DILUTION ASSAY

In ordinary chemical analysis, the compound to be assayed must be isolated from its environment in a pure state and in its entirety. Take as an example the gravimetric assay of sulfate in a solution. Barium chloride is added, and barium sulfate forms and precipitates. The precipitate is purified (that is, freed from other salts and moisture), and weighed. From the weight, the amount of sulfate in the original solution can be calculated. Now, the requirements for success in this simple assay are: absolute purity and complete recovery. If the precipitate of barium sulfate should also contain a little barium carbonate as an impurity, the result would obviously be wrong. If some of the barium sulfate were lost in the filtration and complete recovery were not achieved, the assay would be incorrect. By contrast, an assay performed by the isotope dilution method can dispense with the second condition: complete recovery is not required. Absolute purity still remains the paramount condition. An enormous advantage is gained by an assay method in which 100% recovery is not necessary, in which, in fact, 99% or more of the sample may be lost in the purification procedure. This is because purification is always accompanied by some loss of sample, so that the two conditions of purity and recovery work against each other. In the isotope dilution procedure, one can almost completely ignore recovery and concentrate on purity alone. The theory behind it is the following.

Suppose you have a radioactive solution in a flask containing y mg. of the compound to be analyzed, with specific activity of S_0 c.p.m. per mg. Now you add unlabeled carrier of weight G mg. to the solution, the carrier being, of course, the same compound as the labeled material. The unlabeled G mixes homogeneously in solution with the labeled y. The labeled material therefore has been diluted with unlabeled carrier and will then have a new specific activity of S c.p.m. per mg. But since only unlabeled carrier was added, *total radioactivity* in the flask before addition of carrier is obviously the same as total radioactivity after addition. Now, by definition:

$$\text{Specific activity} = \frac{\text{Total activity}}{\text{Weight}}$$

Therefore:

$$\text{Total activity} = \text{Specific activity} \times \text{Weight}$$

Then:

$$\underset{\substack{\text{Specific} \\ \text{activity}}}{S_0} \times \underset{\text{Weight}}{y} = \underset{\substack{\text{New specific} \\ \text{activity}}}{S} \times \underset{\text{New weight}}{(y + G)}$$

Total activity before dilution = Total activity after dilution
(Fundamental isotope dilution equation)

Take the simplest case: y is negligibly small compared to G. This is a situation commonly encountered in practice:

for instance, a solution contains many labeled amino acids, amongst them a minute amount of labeled glutamic acid ($y = 0.1$ mg.). What is the total radioactivity of this glutamic acid? Carrier glutamic acid ($G = 100$ mg.) is added. Then y becomes negligible compared to G, since, for the purposes of this assay, $(y + G) = 100.01$ mg. can be regarded as simply $G = 100$ mg. The carrier is mixed with the labeled amino acids, and is then re-isolated and purified. Much of it may be lost in this process, so long as S, the new specific activity of the glutamic acid, can be determined by weighing a small sample and counting it. Therefore, S and G are known, and the total activity of the glutamic acid in the mixture ($S_0 \times y$) can be calculated from the above equation, without ever isolating it, except with carrier:

$$(S_0 \times y) = S \times G$$

If by some means (such as the isotope derivative method, see below) one can determine S_0, the specific activity of the material to be assayed, then one can add carrier, G, determine the new specific activity, S, and calculate y, the weight of the radioactive compound. Since

$$S_0 \times y = S \times (y + G)$$

hence:

$$y = \frac{SG}{S_0 - S}$$

9. Reverse Isotope Dilution Assay

The reverse procedure consists in determining the amount of a particular unlabeled compound in solution (G), by adding labeled compound (y) to the solution. For instance: a sample of blood plasma has in it G mg. of cholesterol (unlabeled). One adds to it y mg. of labeled cholesterol (which can be purchased, with known specific activity S_0). The labeled cholesterol mixes with the unlabeled cholesterol of the plasma and becomes diluted. It is then extracted and purified. Only a minute fraction of this mixture needs to be obtained for a specific activity (S) determination. Since S_0, y, and S are now known, the amount of cholesterol in the plasma, G, can be calculated by rearrangement of the fundamental isotope dilution equation:

$$G = \frac{y(S_0 - S)}{S}$$

10. ISOTOPE DERIVATIVE ASSAY

If the analyst is faced with a mixture of small amounts of known *unlabeled* compounds and wants to determine the weight of one of them in the mixture, he can use the Isotope Derivative Method. Suppose the investigator has minute amounts of (unlabeled) fatty acids mixed in solution and wants to assay for one of them, say, palmitic acid. He reacts the mixture with C^{14}-diazomethane of known specific activity. *All* the fatty acids including, of course, the palmitic acid will be converted to their C^{14}-methyl esters (the "isotope derivatives"). Since the acids themselves were originally unlabeled, and have now become labeled by reaction with C^{14}-reagent, the only radioactivity which they contain is from that reagent. Therefore, the specific activity of the methyl esters must be the same as that of the reagent, which is known (S_0). Now unlabeled carrier *derivative* (methyl palmitate) is added in known amount (G), enough to facilitate isolation and purification. The isolated, diluted derivative is then assayed for specific activity (S). As was mentioned, the amount of the original fatty acid (palmitic acid, y), can be calculated by rearrangement of the isotope dilution equation:

$$y = \frac{SG}{S_0 - S}$$

The procedure is further illustrated below:

Mixture
Palmitic acid (y mg.)⎫
Stearic acid   ⎬ + $C^{14}H_2N_2$
Oleic acid   ⎭   Diazomethane
              (specific activity S_0)

$$\rightarrow$$

C^{14}-methyl palmitate ⎫
C^{14}-methyl stearate   ⎬ + methyl palmitate $\rightarrow$
C^{14}-methyl oleate   ⎭   (G mg.)
(specific activity S_0)

             C^{14}-methyl palmitate + methyl palmitate
                      isolated and purified
                    (specific activity S)

The amount of palmitic acid (y) may be minutely small, in fact undeterminable by ordinary chemical analysis. The amount of carrier (G), methyl palmitate, may be large enough to permit easy isolation and purification. This method, which can be applied to almost any type of un-labeled compound even if present in complex mixtures, by correct choice of the labeled derivative, therefore subjects the whole range of analytical chemistry to the great power of the isotope dilution technique.

Section II. Paper Chromatography and Autoradiography

Autoradiography has found application in two distinct ways: (*a*) the process of making visible radioactive spots on paper chromatograms by exposure to photographic film; (*b*) the process of making visible (on a microscopic scale) radioactive substances located within cell structures by exposure of histological sections to photographic film. The technique is one of the earliest used in detection and determination of radioactivity, dating back to the discovery of radioactivity itself, by Becquerel (1896), when a uranium-containing mineral was accidentally placed near some photographic plates and found to have made a picture of itself on the emulsion. It depends on the fact that ionizing radiation (as well as light) can cause a change or sensitization in the silver salts of a photographic emulsion. This change is made apparent upon "developing," when the sensitized silver salt grains are reduced to metallic silver which shows up black wherever radiation (or light) has interacted with the film.

Obviously, one would wish to blacken only a few grains in the emulsion with each radioactive atom, so as to obtain good resolution or, in other words, a sharp image. This is obtained with H^3 (tritium). Its β-rays have such low energy (0.019 Mev. maximum energy) that their range is short: only 1–2 silver salt grains are blackened by each emitting atom. Therefore, when labeled with tritium, microscopically small particles within cells (e.g., chromosomes) can appear sharply defined. This is not so with C^{14} or S^{35} (0.155 Mev. maximum energy), though they have also been used in autoradiography. P^{32} (1.72 Mev. maximum energy) gives only blurred pictures, and pure γ-emitters cannot be used for autoradiography.

1. Radioactive Compounds Separated by Paper Chromatography

The technique of paper chromatography, invented and developed just in time to be of use in radioisotope chemistry and biology, seems as though tailor-made for the purpose. Briefly, it consists in the application of a small amount of a mixture of compounds (labeled or unlabeled) in a spot to a sheet of filter paper near one end. A solvent mixture is passed through the paper by capillary action, starting at the end near the spot. The compounds in the mixture move through the paper with the solvent, each at a different rate characteristic of the chemical properties of the compound and the solvent mixture. They thus form

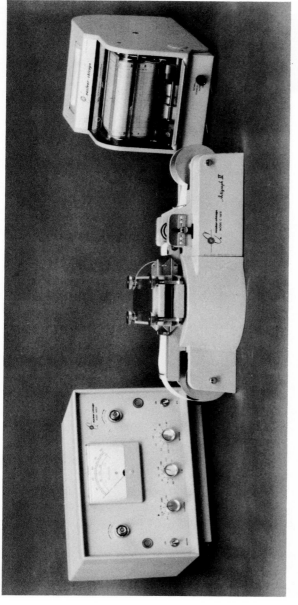

Fig. 4. Paper chromatogram scanner. On left, ratemeter; in center, paper chromatogram strip passing through Geiger counter; on right, recorder tracing radioactive spots as peaks on chart. (Courtesy of Nuclear Chicago Corp.)

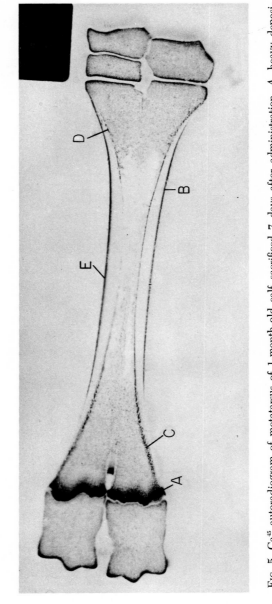

FIG. 5. Ca^{45} autoradiogram of metatarsus of 1-month-old calf sacrificed 7 days after administration. A, heavy deposition below epiphyseal plate; B, sharp subperiosteal deposition; C, spotty deposition in area of endochondral bone growth; D, trabecular bone; E, compact bone of shaft. [From C. L. Comar, "Radioisotopes in Biology and Agriculture," p. 343. McGraw-Hill, New York, 1955.]

84

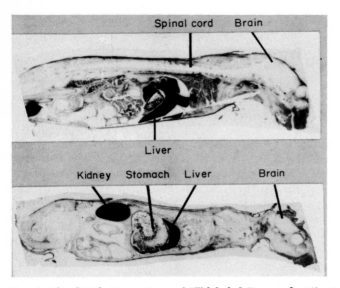

FIG.. 6. The distribution pattern of I^{131}-labeled Renografin 15 minutes after injection. Note that the drug does not penetrate into the central nervous system. Kidney shows very high concentration. [From V. Nair and L. J. Roth. *Advan. Tracer Methodol.* **1**, 309 (1963).]

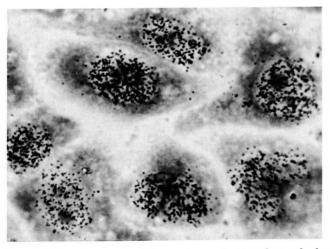

FIG. 7. Photomicrograph of tissue slice and autoradiograph showing concentration of thymidine in nuclei. (Courtesy Division of Biophysics, Sloan-Kettering Institute, New York.) [From J. Weinstein, (*New Engl. Nuclear "Atomlight,"* June (1958).]

a series of spots along the paper where the solvent has moved. The ratio of the distance traversed by a given compound over that traversed by the solvent mixture is known as the R_f, and is a useful physical constant of that compound.

When the solvent has dried, the spots on the paper can be made visible by a spray that will develop a color with the compounds in the spots, or by their appearance in ultraviolet light, or by their radioactivity. The radioactivity of the spots may have been present in the compounds in the original mixture applied to the paper; or it may be produced in the spots by spraying the paper with a radioactive reagent, which reacts with the compounds in the spots and thus makes them radioactive (excess unreacted reagent, of course, must be removed from the paper).

To make the radioactive spots visible, the paper is exposed to sheets of film (X-ray film)—wherever there is radioactivity on the paper, a black spot appears on the film.

As an alternative, the paper may be passed under a Geiger counter arranged in such a way as to give a summation of all the counts per minute at any one spot (rate meter, see Chap. I, Sect. 6). This instrument then registers this information on a chart in the form of a graph, the peaks of which correspond to the radioactive spots on the paper (Fig. 4). The area under each peak is proportional to the amount of radioactivity in the corresponding spot. Alternatively, the spot can be dissolved from the paper ("eluted") and counted, or the radioactivity can be assayed by counting the compound directly on the paper.

It is clear from the above that paper chromatography is an ideal technique for radiochemistry: small amounts of material can be quantitatively separated, and radiochemical purity can be checked, since small amounts of radioactive impurities are readily separated and detected. To establish the identity of a radioactive compound, the coincidence of peaks between nonradioactive carrier, chromatographed on paper along with the radioactive compound, can be observed. A high degree of confidence in the identity is attainable if this coincidence of peaks is found upon chromatography with a wide variety of solvent mixtures. Ultimately, the radioactive spot can be eluted from the paper and crystallized with the carrier to constant specific activity, as described (Chap. V, Sect. I-1).

2. TISSUE AUTORADIOGRAPHY

Autoradiography can be applied with much greater scope to tissues and histological specimens than to paper chromatograms. This technique began with observations on whole tissues, was extended to microscopic studies with cells, and has now reached the level of subcellular entities, in particular the chromosomes.

At the tissue level, autoradiography has revealed the pattern of calcification of bone. The labeled calcium salt ($Ca^{45}Cl_2$) is given to sets of growing animals, which are then killed at given intervals. Thin longitudinal sections of bone are exposed to film. Black areas on the film reveal places in the bone where the calcium salts have been deposited (Fig. 5), and therefore show the location of new bone growth.

Intestinal wall exposed at different times after feeding a labeled amino acid showed the distribution of the compound absorbed in the various parts of the tissue in the process of absorption. Translocation of mineral nutrients taken up by plants could be followed simply by pressing the plant onto film, after it had taken up the labeled minerals. This technique has been adapted to animals (Nair and Roth, 1963) and is termed "whole-body autoradiography." It makes possible the study of the distribution of a radioactive drug throughout the whole body at once, rather

than in isolated, separated organs, and shows up compartmentalization of the drug, such as its confinement to blood
vessels, or the pathways of its excretion. A mouse is injected with the labeled drug and killed after the desired
time has elapsed. It is immediately frozen in dry ice–
acetone. The whole carcass is then sectioned right across,
from head to tail, by a cold microtome to give longitudinal
histological sections of the whole animal, which can be
stained and then exposed to film. The pictures obtained
show cross sections of the whole animal, with liver, heart,
brain, etc. clearly visible (Fig. 6) and blackened according
to the amount of radioactive drug taken up.

3. CELL AUTORADIOGRAPHY

At the level of the cell, a great deal of work has been
done on the incorporation of labeled metabolites into particular cells or part of cells. For instance, labeled glycine
injected into a rat appears in certain cells of the liver, and
in subcellular structures in the course of being incorporated
into protein. Very thin sections of the liver, embedded in
wax, are made, placed on microscope slides, and stained.
The stain makes visible the cell types and parts of cells for
microscopic examination. A special type of film ("stripping
film emulsion") is now placed over the tissue section. This
film is an exceedingly thin layer of light-sensitive small-
grain photographic emulsion (4μ thick; $1 \mu = 0.001$ milli-
meter), supported by a layer of gelatin (10μ). The film
strip is floated on water, emulsion side down, and can be
scooped up onto the slide to cover the histological specimen. Those cells or parts of cells containing radioactive
atoms blacken the emulsion lying upon it, after exposure
for several days. When looked at through the microscope,
one sees: (1) the outline of all the cell structures, shown
by the stain in the section itself; (2) on top of it, those
parts which are radioactive, as black spots in the overlying
emulsion (Fig. 7).

4. CHROMOSOME AUTORADIOGRAPHY

The most important contribution that this technique has made to biology has been in the field of the chemistry of the chromosome and the cell nucleus. Whereas it is possible, on the one hand, to obtain a good picture of chromosome behavior by simple staining and microscopy, it will be a static one, giving information only about the moment when the stain was applied. On the other hand, it is possible to perform metabolic experiments with extracts of broken-up tissue. These extracts contain the essential chemicals for the genetic function of the chromosomes: deoxyribonucleic acid (DNA), ribonucleic acid (RNA), protein. The enzymatic reactions performed by the genetic substances can thus be investigated. However, the structures have to be broken and the spatial organization of the chemical substances concerned thereby destroyed. Yet this spatial organization is a necessary factor in the interactions of these giant molecules.

The autoradiographic technique has combined the virtues of the histological approach with those of the metabolic method. Data on the chemistry of the chromosomes and cell nuclei can be obtained in the course of their growth, division, and rearrangements, in a rapid and easy manner.

This technique was greatly aided by the use of labeled hydrogen (H^3 or tritium or T). Its maximum energy (0.019 Mev.) is so low that its range in the emulsion is only 2 microns. Over 90% of its radiation is released in a sphere of 0.5-micron radius. This is so small that for each molecule containing T atoms, only one grain of silver salt is blackened. It is therefore possible to recognize the position of a labeled molecule within a chromosome segment of no greater dimension than 1 micron. Furthermore, T-labeled compounds can be made easily and cheaply, with high specific activity, by the Wilzbach procedure (Chap. I,

Sect. 8). One compound in particular, thymidine, which is especially susceptible to this labeling technique, is exclusively incorporated into DNA, the substance unique to the chromosomes.

The problem to be solved was: chromosomes are fibers made of DNA, RNA, and protein; how do these components behave when a chromosome divides in the course of cell division?

The classical experiment was that of Taylor *et al.* (1957). This has since been taken up and greatly expanded by many other investigators. Roots of the English broad bean were grown in mineral solution containing T-labeled thymidine for 8 hours, or ⅓ of a division cycle. The nuclei in the cells of this plant have 12 clearly visible, large chromosomes. The roots were then transferred to a solution of colchicine, but containing no labeled compounds. Colchicine has the property of preventing division of cells and nuclei without interrupting chromosome division. The root segments were then squashed onto microscope slides, fixed, stained with a dye showing up the DNA, and covered with photographic emulsion. After exposure and development, the following observations were made.

Cells in which the chromosomes remained undivided showed 12 chromosomes in their nuclei. Cells having undergone one division cycle were not split into two (because of the effect of colchicine), but nonetheless had 24 chromosomes. Cells which had undergone 2 replications (suppressed divisions) contained 48 chromosomes. Each chromosome, as had been discovered long ago by simple histological staining techniques, is actually made of two sister strands (chromatids), lying closely side by side. On cell division, they are pulled apart and each forms part of the chromosome of the new cell.

In the labeling experiment, those cells with 12 chromosomes all had both chromatid strands labeled. In other words, the DNA component of their chromosomes had taken up labeled thymidine from the medium. Those cells with 24 chromosomes, that is, those which divided while in the *unlabeled* solution, also had every chromosome labeled. But on closer inspection, they presented the following picture: seen under the microscope, both strands of every chromosome were of course stained with the dye taken up by the DNA. But the row of black dots caused by the radioactivity was superimposed over only *one* strand for each chromosome (Fig. 8); in other words, only *one* of

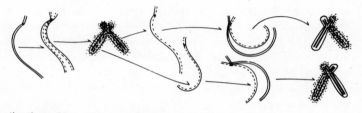

| duplication with labeled thymidine | 1st c-metaphase after labeling | duplication without labeled thymidine | 2nd c-metaphase after labeling |

FIG. 8. Diagrammatic representation of proposed organization and mode of replication which would produce the result seen in the autoradiographs. The two units necessary to explain the results are shown, although these were not resolved by microscopic examination. Solid lines represent nonlabeled units, while those in dashed lines are labeled. The dots represent grains in the autoradiographs. [From J. H. Taylor *et al., Proc. Natl. Acad. Sci. U. S.* **43**, 122 (1957).]

the sister chromatid strands was labeled. This was interpreted to mean that, after the labeled chromatid strands had pulled away from their labeled sister strands, a newly synthesized unlabeled DNA strand was paired with each of the labeled parent chromatids. It also means that the DNA strands remained intact during division.

In cells with 48 chromosomes, the picture was again quite different. Here, not all chromosomes were labeled. Upon counting the number that were radioactive, it was found that just half of the 48 were labeled and half not.

Those that were labeled, again, had one nonradioactive strand and one strand with label.

This amazingly clear-cut and elegant result demonstrated . that during the second replication cycle, again, each chromosome was pulled apart. Each of the two chromatid strands of every chromosome formed a new chromosome. In the course of the first replication, one strand had become labeled and one was unlabeled. Now, in the second division, the unlabeled sister paired with a newly synthesized unlabeled strand. The labeled sister strand also paired with unlabeled DNA. Therefore, after the second replication, one chromosome was labeled and one unlabeled. Hence, in the picture, half the chromosomes were radioactive, half not. Those that were labeled had one radioactive chromatid strand and one unlabeled.

Here, for the first time, we witnessed the chemical changes in chromosomes during division. The final conclusions were: chromosomes are made of two strands of DNA, each of which on division behaves as a complete entity, remaining intact during successive replications. During replication, each new chromosome receives one chromatid strand from the original chromosome and one new strand. Newly built DNA, therefore, does not go randomly into the new chromosome, but rather forms a new entity, paired with the old one.

These conclusions are a triumphant proof for the Watson-Crick hypothesis (see Chap. VI, Sect. II-8) of how the genetic information contained in the DNA is copied out by the cell and handed on to its daughter.

The autoradiographic experiments of Taylor and his team have been expanded to other plants, to bacteria, amoebae, insects, and mammals, in order to test the universality of the underlying concept. Even human chromosomes from cells in tissue culture have been studied by this technique. Such problems as the point at which DNA replication starts on each chromatid strand, and the time of replication, are being answered.

REFERENCES

Arnstein, H. R. V., and Grant, P. T. (1957). *Progr. in Biophys.* **7**, 178.

Calvin, M. and Bassham, J. A. (1957). "The Path of Carbon in Photosynthesis." Prentice-Hall, Englewood Cliffs, New Jersey.

Calvin, M., and Bassham, J. A. (1962). "The Photosynthesis of Carbon Compounds." W. A. Benjamin, New York.

Gautschi, F., and Bloch, K. (1957). *J. Am. Chem. Soc.* **79**, 684.

Gautschi, E., and Bloch, K. (1958). *J. Biol. Chem.* **233**, 1343.

Heidelberger, C., and Wiest, W. G. (1951). *Cancer Res.* **11**, 511.

Nair, V., and Roth, L. J. (1963). *Advan. Tracer Methodol.* **1**, 309.

Newman, H. A. I., and Zilversmit, D. B. (1962). *J. Biol. Chem.* **237**, 2078.

Taylor, J. H., Woods, P. S., and Hughes, W. L. (1957). *Proc. Natl. Acad. Sci. U. S.* **43**, 122.

VI

Application of the
Isotope Technique

Section I. Gross Distribution Studies

By "Gross Distribution" is meant the distribution of elements or compounds in different locations, from the geographical level down to the level of the cell. It simply determines the *movement* of elements or compounds. This concept is in distinction to "Molecular Distribution" (to be discussed later), which signifies the distribution of an isotopic element or compound amongst the metabolites to which it is related, and into which it is changed. It determines the *metabolic fate* of the element or compound.

1. GEOGRAPHICAL DISTRIBUTION

In the simplest case of gross distribution studies, the isotope is not used as a chemical entity, but rather as a physical "tag" attached to the organism. Radioactive cobalt (Co^{60}), for instance, has been placed in the body cavity of wireworm larvae, and their location and movement underground followed by the emission of the penetrating γ-rays onto the surface. Entomologists have made studies of flight and dispersion, of feeding and breeding habits of insects, by feeding them radioactive phosphorus (P^{32}), and following the radioactive flies, mosquitoes, or cockroaches by radiation detectors. Mosquito larvae, for example, were given P^{32}-labeled phosphate, hatched, and released. The "labeled" mosquitoes mixed with the unlabeled ones in the given area. After a predetermined time, traps were set up and mosquitoes collected. Knowing the radioactivity per labeled mosquito (its "specific activity"), and the total radioactivity per trap, it is then possible to tell by how many unlabeled mosquitoes the labeled ones were "diluted." From the dilution factor, the mosquito population of the area can be calculated. This is an example of an isotope dilution experiment exactly like those described for labeled compounds (Chap. V, Sect. I-8).

In a recent study, capsules containing a solution of radioactive iodide were placed under the skin of one of a community of field mice living in a blue-grass field. The labeled mouse was released, and its movement followed and mapped daily by locating it at given times by means of a Geiger counter fixed to a long pole. Radioactive iodine (I^{131}) has the advantage of being a high-energy emitter, so that the radiation penetrates through layers of soil. Further, its half-life is only 8.1 days, so that in case the mouse should escape, the radioactivity would rapidly decay to safe levels. At the end of the experiment, the mouse was caught again, by use of the counter, and the capsule removed.

2. TRANSLOCATION

The next step down from these large-scale studies of the movement of animals in their environment, is the study of the movement of nutrients from the soil into plants, and their translocation within the plants. So for instance, as was explained (Chap. V, Sect. II-2), the uptake of P^{32}-labeled phosphate by the roots of plants was investigated by autoradiography. Taking samples of the plant at different times and exposing them to X-ray film, it was discovered that the upward movement in translocation of minerals took place within water-conducting elements of the plant, the subsequent downward movement in the phloem elements. A parallel area of investigation in animals is the uptake of labeled nutrients across the walls of the intestine.

3. DRUG DISTRIBUTION

Closely related is the study of the uptake and distribution of labeled pesticides, and the movement and organ distribution of drugs within animal bodies. This type of study has assumed great importance recently in the effort towards protection of the consumer public against harmful effects of new drugs. The Food and Drug Administration now requires companies to provide experimental proof to demonstrate that newly introduced food preparations or drugs are not toxic or harmful. Whereas in pre-isotope days, it would have taken years to determine whether a drug has harmful side effects by performing prolonged toxicity tests, it is now possible sometimes to decide the matter within days. This enables industrial firms testing new drugs rapidly to demonstrate their harmlessness to the satisfaction of the F.D.A. For instance: it had been discovered in the early 1950's that the synthetic female sex hormone, diethylstilbestrol, when fed to steers, caused greatly improved weight gains and meat quality. The question had to be settled whether this compound might contaminate the meat and thus exert its hormonal influence on people eating it. H^3-labeled diethylstilbestrol was fed to steers in the usual way. After slaughter, the meat was analyzed. Over 50% of the radioactivity had been excreted in urine and feces. Lean meat contained 0.3 part per billion, fat 0.35, and liver 9.12 parts per billion of the hormone, as determined by radioactivity. These quantities are so minutely small that, quite probably, they are comparable to the amount of naturally occurring sex hormones present in ordinary untreated meat. The case was therefore clearly proved that the hormone could be safely fed to livestock, since the compounds simply do not penetrate to the parts of the animal which are eaten.

Complete patterns of absorption from the intestine, transfer from the circulation to the tissues, tissue distribution, excretion through kidney and urine or through bile and feces, can all be ascertained rapidly in drug evaluation studies with radioactive drugs. The time that a drug remains unchanged and the determination of the number and type of compound it changes into, in the process of its action or detoxication, can be found out readily with labeled drugs. Drug efficacy, in the sense of how much of it reaches the target organ, can be investigated. For example, ointment bases of different fats influence the absorption of the active ingredients of ointments: lanolin caused the fastest absorption of radioactive sodium chloride ($Na^{24}Cl$) through the skin, in a series of ointment bases which were compared.

4. WHOLE-BODY RADIOGRAPHY

A new branch of science has developed around the gross distribution studies of radioactive isotopes in intact tissues of animals and man, measured with instruments outside their bodies. The counters are placed in precisely defined positions on the skin of those parts of the body to be investigated, and definition of the "image" is sharpened by suitable shielding. Corrections can be made for scattering and absorption, and for "geometry" losses (that is, for the loss of radiation that occurs when the counter is placed in such a position that it cannot "see" all the counts emitted by the labeled source within the organ). Iodine-131, a γ-emitting isotope of iodine, has proved especially useful in these distribution studies. Its half-life is short (8.1 days), and its radiation penetrates tissues without great losses.

Studies of this sort have been applied mostly to thyroid function. The thyroid gland makes a hormone, thyroxine, which is the only iodine-containing compound in the body. If a test dose of radioactive iodine is given, some of it rapidly concentrates in the thyroid gland. The rest is excreted. Hyperthyroid individuals take up about 50%, and normal persons only 10–20% of a test dose in 24 hours. In this way thyroid function can be rapidly checked, as well as the extent and patterns of various diseases which affect this gland.

An interesting application of radioactive iodine distribution is in the diagnosis of brain tumors. These growths possess the peculiar property of selectively taking up the drug fluorescein from the bloodstream. If this drug is iodinated with I^{131} (i.e., iodine atoms are attached to the molecule of the drug), to form radioactive diiodofluorescein, this compound is equally well concentrated by the tumor. It is then possible to identify and to locate the tumor precisely within the brain, through the γ-radiation emitted by the drug, with a counter on the skull. This procedure is of great value in diagnosis and subsequent surgery.

Intestinal absorption and distribution studies have been made with iodinated plasma proteins. Here the intact protein, when brought in contact with iodine, takes up some of this element, presumably on the aromatic rings of the amino acids phenylalanine and tyrosine. If the iodine is radioactive, labeled plasma proteins can be made. The iodinated proteins can be expected on the whole to behave much like normal proteins in their gross distribution throughout the circulatory system, but it must be remembered that they would show different properties from normal proteins in their metabolic behavior.

5. "Volume" and "Space" Determinations

With iodinated plasma proteins, not only their distribution, but also the plasma volumes of different organs—liver, lungs, brain—can be determined. The principle again is that of the isotope dilution method (Chap. V, Sect. I-8). A small amount of highly labeled plasma protein of known specific radioactivity, small enough in weight not to disturb the normal plasma protein concentration, is injected. After equilibration has taken place (a few minutes), the dilution of its radioactivity is measured by withdrawing a sample and determining the new specific radioactivity. Suppose 8 mg. of plasma protein of specific radioactivity of 50,000 c.p.m. per mg. is injected into a rat and, after mixing and withdrawal, its specific activity is 500 c.p.m. per mg. Therefore, the dilution is 100-fold, and the amount of total plasma protein in the circulation present at the moment of injection must be 8 mg. $\times$ 100, or 800 mg. Now, if the concentration of plasma protein, as determined chemically just before the moment of injection, was 80 mg. per ml., then the total volume over which 800 mg. of protein was distributed would be (800 mg.)/(80 mg./ml.) = 10 ml., which is then known as the *plasma protein space*.

Similar experiments were carried out with C^{14}-glucose in an eviscerated rabbit. The glucose space in the rabbit was found to be 570 ml. This volume is not large enough to include the cell mass of the animal, but only the circulation and extracellular fluid. The conclusion was that blood glucose does not equilibrate with intracellular glucose. It is taken up and utilized by the cells, but does not again move out of the cells.

6. Radiocardiology

In a similar manner, red blood cells can be labeled by incubating them with radioactive chromium (as sodium dichromate), and re-injecting them into the circulation; the volume of the vascular system can then be calculated from the dilution of their radioactivity, after thorough mixing and distribution. Indeed, the study of blood circulation, by external counting of radioactive sodium (as $Na^{24}Cl$), has given much information not obtainable by other means. The isotopic compound is injected into a blood vessel in one part of the body, and the time of its appearance at another is measured. It was found that the time of transfer of blood from the upper arm to the hand was 11 seconds; from arm to arm, 18 seconds. In patients with heart disease, this time was much longer. Local clearance of $Na^{24}Cl$ was measured by determining disappearance of the isotope. When injected into muscle, it was cleared mostly through the blood, only 1% being carried away by the lymphatic system. Effects of tourniquets and drugs on clearance were also studied.

By placing counters simultaneously over the heart and over different parts of the body, and observing distribution of radioactivity after injection of isotope, "mixing time" throughout the body could be determined. Though some tissues lagged a little behind the liver and heart, mixing generally was complete within the short time of 2 minutes. This method was expanded into "radiocardiology." Radioactive sodium chloride is injected into an arm vein. Two shielded Geiger counters are placed over the right and left sides, of the heart, respectively. They are connected together to a recorder which traces their output with a pen on a chart of moving paper, producing a graph. When a "wave" of the isotope reaches the right side of the heart, the first peak is obtained. This decreases as the blood, containing the isotope, leaves again to pass through the lungs. Finally, a second peak appears, as the labeled wave arrives at the left chamber of the heart, from where it is then slowly emptied. Thus, in the normal radiocardiogram, two characteristic peaks and a valley between are traced, each with its normal time span. In patients with heart enlargements, the time for the peaks is prolonged. In congestive heart failure, there is a more gradual rise of the waves and obscuring of the valley between the peaks. An interesting variety of information can be thus obtained, entirely different in principle from the electrocardiogram.

7. Organ and Cell Distribution

In gross distribution studies of drugs or other types of compound such as vitamins, it is sometimes useful to obtain an organ distribution expressed as a specific activity. This

TABLE I

Concentration of Activity in Tissues after C^{14}-Carotene Administration[a,b]

Tissue	Fraction[c]	Hours after dosing							
		1	2	4	6	10	16	22	28
Adrenals	N.S.	N.a.[d]	223.6	259.0	431.8	1041.6	406.0	221.0	144.9
	Sap.	−	+	10.3	79.0	72.7	50.9	110.0	91.6
Heart	N.S.	0.405	0.360	0.851	0.849	0.530	0.751	0.540	−
	Sap.	0.420	0.236	0.326	0.454	0.851	0.555	0.541	0.255
Hypophysis	N.S.	3.874	2.165	4.651	14.505	2.406	3.431	3.727	5.333
	Sap.	+	3.878	6.977	23.750	+	10.032	+	+
Intestines	N.S.	N.a.†	1.674	2.182	3.394	1.735	0.379	0.461	−
	Sap.	0.323	−	0.627	−	−	−	−	−
Kidneys	N.S.	0.255	0.338	0.571	0.904	0.882	0.955	1.059	0.785
	Sap.	−	0.574	−	−	0.192	−	−	0.137
Liver	N.S.	0.567	0.470	2.369	1.812	4.080	3.654	4.154	1.919
	Sap.	0.282	0.205	0.330	0.355	0.380	0.715	0.205	0.231
Lungs	N.S.	−	−	+	+	1.468	1.735	1.903	1.059
	Sap.								
Spleen	N.S.	0.195	+	0.228	0.252	0.415	0.241	+	+
	Sap.								
Stomach	N.S.	0.585	0.316	0.221	−	−	−	−	−
	Sap.	−	−	−	+	+	+	−	−
Blood (c.p.m./ml.)	N.S.	0.166	0.312	0.237	0.094	0.153	0.105	0.123	0.100
	Sap.	+	+	+	+	+	−	+	+

[a] From J. S. Willmer and D. H. Laughland, *Can. J. Biochem. Physiol.* **35**, 819 (1957).
[b] Counts per minute per gm. tissue $\times 10^{-3}$; +, trace of radioactivity; −, no radioactivity.
[c] N.S., nonsaponifiable (mostly vitamin A); Sap., saponifiable.
[d] Result not available.

has been done for C^{14}-carotene, demonstrating a high concentration of Vitamin A in the adrenal glands, when expressed as radioactivity per gram of tissue, though the total radioactivity in the gland may be quite low (Table I). This observation has led to some fruitful researches on the involvement of vitamin A in adrenal cortex function.

Lastly, we arrive at a discussion of isotope distribution at the level of the cell. By high-speed centrifugation, the various structures within the cell: nucleus, mitochondria, microsomes, and supernatant solution or cell sap, can be separated from each other. It is then possible to determine the distribution of radioactive metabolites, hormones, vitamins, or drugs in these cell fractions, and relate their concentration in one particular fraction to their function, since many of the functions performed by these cell fractions are now well understood. When, for instance, the carcinogen dibenzanthracene labeled with C^{14} was injected into the submaxillary gland, the distribution of radioactivity bound to protein of subcellular fractions was found to be as shown in Table II.

However, ultimately these gross distribution studies can give only a guideline to further work. Rarely are they of

TABLE II

DISTRIBUTION OF RADIOACTIVITY IN THE SUBMAXILLARY GLAND[a,b]

Cell Fraction	Total C^{14} (c.p.m.)	Protein-bound C^{14}	
		Total activity (c.p.m.)	Specific activity (c.p.m./μg.)
Homogenate	530,000	—	—
Nuclei	33,000	110	19
Large granules	205,000	675	58
Small granules	23,000	35	9
Soluble protein	104,000	290	27

[a] One week after injection of dibenzanthracene-C^{14} 1.2×10^6 c.p.m. in tricaprylin.

[b] From W. G. Wiest and C. Heidelberger, *Cancer Res.* **13**, 246 (1953).

primary importance themselves. Therefore, one ultimately arrives at the molecular level, and at a consideration of molecular distribution of isotopes.

Section II. Molecular Distribution Studies

Radioisotopes, in particular carbon-14 and tritium, have found their greatest usefulness, in an astonishingly wide range of applications, in molecular distribution studies. As pointed out at the beginning of this chapter, the study of molecular distribution is concerned with the fate of a molecule, as it is related to or changed into its metabolites. If one leafs through a recent issue of any biological, in particular any biochemical, journal, one notices that almost three-quarters of the investigations reported depend on C^{14} or H^3. The reason for this dependence is that, as biology becomes more advanced, it concerns itself increasingly with phenomena at the chemical (i.e., molecular) level, where isotopes are generally the most sensitive and potent means of exploration.

For this reason, it is patently impossible to review all, or even all types or groups, of the applications of isotopes to metabolic studies. Only certain experiments, exemplifying certain particularly original, illuminating, or typical applications, will be described.

A. Metabolic Pathways; Biosynthesis and Breakdown

The concept of *the dynamic state of body constituents,* long suspected, was firmly established as long ago as 1940 by the use of the heavy hydrogen isotope by Schoenheimer (1942). Take glucose as an example. The level of blood glucose is constant, but each glucose molecule in the blood has only a short life and is rapidly broken down or removed, only to be replaced by newly formed glucose molecules. The same applies to amino acids, to nearly all proteins, fats, nucleic acids (except the genetic material of the cell, the DNA, which is stable, for obvious reasons, for the life span of each cell), and even to bone tissue. Whether there is an actual physiological need for the breakdown of a body constituent at any given moment or not, it will be broken down and newly formed all the time, at a rate characteristic of the particular compound (its "turnover rate"). It is obvious that only isotopic compounds can be used to study this replacement. Normally, one molecule of glucose looks like any other, whether just added to the blood "pool" or present for some time, whereas isotopic glucose is tagged and can be added to the pool at a given, chosen moment, and its subsequent fate and turnover can be studied.

When it was found that every compound in every living organism is constantly synthesized and broken down, it became a matter of importance to understand the sequence of reactions—the metabolic pathways—of synthesis and breakdown. Beginning with carbon dioxide, fixed by plants into the sugars, amino acids, fats, and the more complex compounds needed for life and eaten by animals and built into their bodies; continuing with their transformations in the animal body; and ending with their breakdown to excretion products: almost all these pathways have been established with the use of isotopes.

1. The Path of Carbon in Photosynthesis

It is not the purpose of this book to describe or discuss the metabolic pathways. However, a number of classical examples will be given to illustrate the methods used. *The path of carbon in photosynthesis* (see the brilliantly lucid article by Bassham, 1962), as Calvin and his collaborators (1957) have termed the reaction sequence serving the fixation of CO_2 by plants, has already been mentioned in a discussion of the "Isotope Dilution Method" (Chap. V, Sect. I). Indeed, this technique, in the form of "trapping" or in many other guises, has been fundamental in the elucidation of metabolic pathways.

The elaboration of carbon compounds, from the simple into the complex, from 1- and 2-carbon compounds to those in which tens of thousands of carbon atoms are lined up together (as in the proteins and nucleic acids), has as its very beginning the conversion of "inorganic" carbon dioxide gas of the atmosphere into "organic" compounds. This is the fixation of CO_2 by plants through the energy of light.

It is significant that CO_2 fixation was the first biological experiment performed with C^{14} in the early 1940's by Kamen and Ruben when they discovered this isotope. The problem was taken up by Calvin and his group in 1946 and led to a highly satisfactory conclusion. From that date, and beginning with CO_2 fixation, the array of interlocking metabolic pathways has been made into the great "metabolic maps" which guide the biologist through our biochemical world.

Light energy interacts with chlorophyll in the chloro-plasts, the small organs within the plant cells which contain the photosynthetic apparatus. By a process not yet fully understood, this energy is used to split water into hydrogen and oxygen. The latter is given off as oxygen gas. The oxidation of the former provides the energy for the interaction of carbon dioxide with plant substances, and thus its fixation.

The design of the actual experiments was of a simplicity that is so often the hallmark of a mind of genius. Single-celled green algae were grown in liquid medium in illumi-nated transparent vessels. Labeled CO_2 (in the form of sodium C^{14}-bicarbonate) could be injected into the vessels, and light turned on or off, as required. Samples of algae were withdrawn into hot alcohol, which instantly killed the plants. In this way, extremely short-term experiments could be performed. The plant extract was separated into its constituents by paper chromatography (Chap. V, Sect. II-1). Autoradiography of the paper chromatograms revealed the distribution of radioactivity in the compounds extracted. In 30 seconds a large number of compounds, both sugars and amino acids, had become labeled. By reducing the time of exposure to $C^{14}O_2$ and light to 5 seconds, principally only one compound was formed. By carrier and isotope dilution techniques (Chap. V, Sect. I-1), this was identified as 3-phosphoglyceric acid (PGA). It was chemically split up (degraded) into separate compounds derived from carbons 1, 2, and 3. Radioactivity was

(3) CH_2OPO_3H
     |
(2) $CHOH$
     |
(1) CO_2H
     3-PGA

detected in the compound from carbon 1 only. Obviously, the free $C^{14}O_2$ had been added to some compound in the course of the fixation reaction to produce the PGA. This, then, was the first reaction of photosynthesis: the combination of CO_2 with another compound to give PGA, which then was converted to sugars and amino acids. The energy and "reducing power" of the hydrogen formed in the primary light reaction from water is used for these conversions. Which, now, is the compound that *accepts* CO_2? When $C^{14}O_2$ was added in the dark, the labeled ,PGA accumulated, as it was no longer converted to other sugars. To the extent that C^{14} in PGA accumulated, the radioactivity of one, and only one, compound present in the plant extract decreased under these circumstances. It was identified as ribulose diphosphate (RDP), a 5-carbon sugar. This signified that, as PGA accumulated, RDP was used up. In other words

$$RDP + CO_2 \rightarrow PGA$$

The photosynthetic cycle was therefore established (Fig. 1):

RDP (5 carbons) + CO_2 → unknown 6-carbon intermediate →
  2 PGA (3 carbons) → triose phosphate (3-carbon sugar)
$$\xrightarrow{\text{2-carbon fragment}} \text{RDP (5 carbons)}$$

By altering conditions: shutting off $C^{14}O_2$ but leaving on the light, doing the experiment over longer periods until a steady state (an equilibrium condition) had been achieved, and many others, a complete picture of all the intermediates in the photosynthetic cycle was obtained.

This example beautifully illustrates a unique facet of the radioisotope technique: it makes possible the study of cyclic reactions. The *amounts* of PGA, RDP, or the other intermediates neither increase nor decrease: there is no net change, CO_2 enters the cycle, sugars leave it. Only by using $C^{14}O_2$ can one follow its progress through the intermediates of the cycle, in terms of their acquisition or loss of radioactivity.

2. THE KREBS CYCLE

The photosynthetic cycle, which serves to convert light energy to storable chemical energy, has its close parallel in another cycle of reactions in which chemical energy is made available and CO_2 released, the Krebs cycle. This is an excellent example of the study of "synthesis in the absence of net synthesis" made possible by the isotope technique.

A 2-carbon compound, acetic acid (derived from sugars and combined with coenzyme A), reacts with oxalacetic acid (4 carbons) to form citric acid (6 carbons). This, with loss of 1 CO_2, yields ketoglutaric acid (5 carbons) which, again by loss of CO_2, gives succinic acid (4 carbons). The last named is converted back to oxalacetic acid, and the cycle begins again (Fig. 2). A 2-carbon compound has entered the cycle of reactions, and 2 CO_2 molecules leave it: no weight is gained, there is no net synthesis. The reactions serve the production of energy which as adenosine triphosphate (ATP) accompanies the liberation of CO_2.

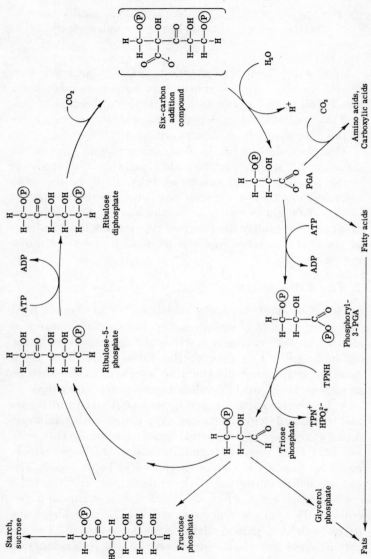

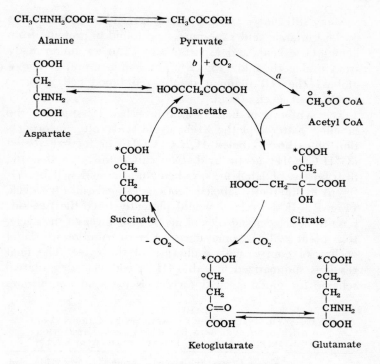

Fig. 2. Krebs tricarboxylic acid cycle.

Though this cycle was discovered without the help of isotopes, its detailed workings, in particular the participation of acetic acid, could be studied only with labeled compounds.

Fig. 1. End products of photosynthesis are not limited to carbohydrates (e.g., sucrose and starch), as first thought, but include, among other things, fatty acids, fats, carboxylic acids and amino acids. Carbon cycle shown here is highly simplified; it involves at least 12 discrete reactions. Moreover, the steps from PGA to fatty acids and to amino and carboxylic acids have not been indicated. [From J. A. Bassham, *Sci. American* **206**, 88 (1962).]

Many substances are derived from members of the Krebs cycle: glutamic acid (an amino acid found in protein) from ketoglutaric acid, and aspartic acid (also an amino acid) from oxalacetic acid (Fig. 2). The hemin group of hemoglobin (the red pigment of the red blood cells) comes partly from succinic acid.

The synthesis of heme was established by studying the labeling patterns of the Krebs cycle acids, after incorporation of carboxyl-labeled (CH_3C^*OOH) or methyl-labeled (C^*H_3COOH) acetic acid. One can readily see that the distribution of label in, say, ketoglutaric acid will be different if differently labeled acetic acid feeds into the cycle (Fig. 2). If the reader would patiently trace the two differently labeled molecules of acetic acid through the cycle, this point will become clear. A redistribution of label occurs, of course, with each turn of the cycle. The final result is summarized in Table III. A complete degradative scheme for glutamic acid (which is in rapid equilibrium

TABLE III

RELATIVE DISTRIBUTION OF C^{14} ACTIVITY IN CARBON ATOMS OF α-KETOGLUTARIC ACID RESULTING FROM UTILIZATION OF C^{14}-LABELED ACETATE IN TRICARBOXYLIC ACID CYCLE[a,b]

	From C^{14}-methyl-labeled acetate (activity of methyl group = 10 c.p.m.)				From C^{14}-carboxyl-labeled acetate (activity of carboxyl group = 10 c.p.m.)			
α-Ketoglutaric acid	Number of cycles in tricarboxylic acid cycle							
	1st	2nd	3rd	∞	1st	2nd	3rd	∞
COOH	0	0	0	0	10	10	10	10
CH₂	10	10	10	10	0	0	0	0
CH₂	0	5	7.5	10	0	0	0	0
C=O	0	5	7.5	10	0	0	0	0
COOH	0	0	2.5	5	0	5	5	5

[a] From S. Shemin and J. Wittenberg, *J. Biol. Chem.* **192**, 315 (1951).
[b] The results are expressed in counts per minute.

with ketoglutaric acid Fig. 2) has been established, whereby the radioactivity (as specific activity) in every carbon atom can be ascertained. This radioactivity distribution is, of course, the same as that in ketoglutaric acid which, in turn, reveals whether the label is derived from carboxyl- or methyl-labeled acetate (Table III). The labeling pattern in ketoglutaric acid, of course, also determines that in succinic acid (and all compounds derived from it), because succinic acid is merely ketoglutaric acid minus CO_2 (Fig. 2). Since acetic acid occupies a central position on the metabolic map, being the starting material for cholesterol and fatty acid synthesis, and the end product of the breakdown of fatty acids and several amino acids, as well as the bridge between sugar metabolism and the Krebs cycle, the degradative analysis of glutamic acid has been of great diagnostic value in the ascertainment of metabolic pathways (cf. the alternative metabolic pathways of pyruvate, as determined by glutamic acid labeling (Chap. VI, Sect. III-8).

3. Biosynthesis of Hemin

To return to the biosynthesis of hemin (Shemin and Wittenberg, 1951; Shemin and Kumin, 1952): the hypothesis was proposed that two molecules of succinic acid (activated by a coenzyme group, R) combine with one of glycine to form the basic pyrrole unit, of which four make up the structure of porphyrin (Fig. 3) (porphyrin + iron → hemin). This ingenious idea was tested with duck red blood cells which have the property of making labeled hemoglobin when incubated with labeled substrates. The porphyrin was isolated and chemically degraded, that is, pulled apart by chemical procedures so that the specific activity of each of its carbon atoms could be determined separately. From α-labeled glycine (Fig. 3), the carbon atoms marked x became labeled. With carboxyl-labeled acetic acid the carbons marked ●, and with methyl-labeled

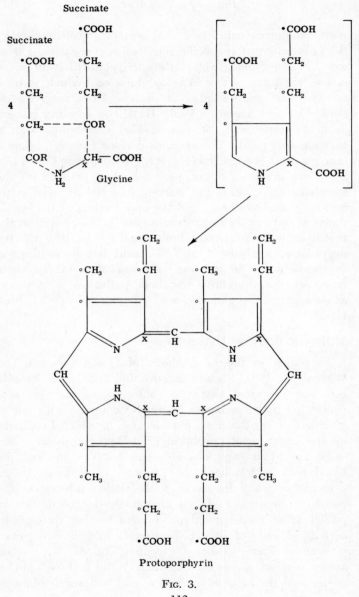

Protoporphyrin

Fɪɢ. 3.

112

acetic acid the carbons marked ○, were labeled. From inspection of Table III, it can be seen that carboxyl-labeled acetic acid gives succinic acid labeled in positions ●, methyl-labeled acetic acid gives succinic acid labeled in positions ○. As can be seen from Fig. 3, these are exactly the positions that would be labeled in hemin if the hypothesis were true that two molecules of succinic acid condense with one of glycine to form the pyrrole rings of porphyrin, as shown. The hypothesis was confirmed by incubating red blood cells with labeled glycine—label then appeared in positions x (Fig. 3). Further experiments with labeled intermediates closer to the final porphyrin completely confirmed this predicted pathway.

4. BIOSYNTHESIS OF CHOLESTEROL

One of the most illuminating examples of isotope methodology in biochemical research concerns the exploration of the biosynthesis of cholesterol by Bloch (Little and Bloch, 1950; Wüersch *et al.*, 1952). This is not strictly a case of using isotopes to demonstrate "synthesis in the absence of net synthesis." However, the extent of synthesis and the concentration of intermediates are so small that in effect only with isotopic precursors was it possible to explore many of the synthetic reactions. Bloch had shown as long ago as the 1940's, with deuterium, that acetic acid (as acetate) is the precursor not only of fatty acids, but also of cholesterol.

Liver slices were incubated with *doubly labeled* acetate, $C^{14}H_3C^{13}OOH$, having a radioactive carbon atom in one position, and a heavy (nonradioactive) carbon atom in the other. The liver slices had the ability to synthesize cholesterol, not of course in weighable amounts, but as measured by isotope uptake into nonisotopic carrier cholesterol. Subsequent chemical degradation revealed that *all* the carbon atoms of cholesterol were derived from acetate, and that *both* carbons of acetate were used in the synthesis. The labeling pattern of the isolated cholesterol could be ex-

plained only if three acetate molecules combined to a
6-carbon compound thus ($C^{14} = \bigcirc$; $C^{13} = x$):

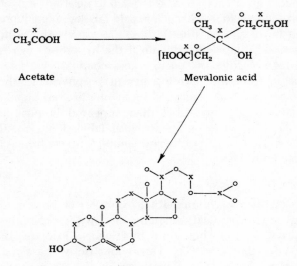

Cholesterol

Cholesterol biosynthesis

The 6-carbon compound was later identified as mevalonic
acid. It loses the carboxyl group (shown in brackets) in
the course of condensation, to form the basic 5-carbon unit
of which the cholesterol skeleton is built up.

Now, in the liver of sharks there occurs an unusual compound, squalene, thought until the 1950's to be nothing
but a strange metabolic aberration. Several organic chemists
had made the suggestion that squalene had the same carbon
skeleton as cholesterol. With this theoretical suggestion in
mind, by an elegant application of the isotope dilution
method, Langdon and Bloch, 1953 used nonradioactive
squalene, obtained from shark liver oil, as a trapping agent
to demonstrate the conversion of acetate to squalene.

Labeled acetate was fed to rats together with unlabeled
squalene. As much as 10% of the amount fed could be re-

isolated from the livers of these rats. When assayed for radioactivity, the re-isolated squalene was found to be labeled. The only way this could have happened was by a process of mixing of the unlabeled squalene fed to the rat with the squalene synthesized by the rat from the labeled acetate. This finding was of the utmost importance: acetate, a simple 2-carbon compound derived from sugars or fats, can be converted to a complex hydrocarbon by liver enzymes:

$$CH_3-\underset{\underset{1}{|}}{\underset{CH_3}{C}}=CHCH_2\!\!+\!\!CH_2-\underset{\underset{2}{|}}{\underset{CH_3}{C}}=CHCH_2\!\!+\!\!CH_2-\underset{\underset{3}{|}}{\underset{CH_3}{C}}=CHCH_2\!\!+\!\!CH_2CH=\underset{\underset{3'}{|}}{\underset{CH_3}{C}}-CH_2\!\!+\!\!CH_2CH=\underset{\underset{2'}{|}}{\underset{CH_3}{C}}-CH_2\!\!+\!\!CH_2CH=\underset{\underset{1'}{|}}{\underset{CH_3}{C}}-CH_3$$

Degradative studies showed that the carbon atoms were again derived from the 5-carbon unit (shown in the cholesterol biosynthesis diagram). Six of these condense together as shown, in symmetrical fashion.

The isolated labeled squalene was used in these experiments not merely as a means for proving that it was synthesized. Some of it was re-fed to other rats. It was found that in these rats the cholesterol was labeled to the extent of 20% of the radioactivity fed as squalene. Thus, the reaction sequence:

acetate → mevalonate → squalene → cholesterol

was proved. The squalene molecule, by a process of folding up and a series of simultaneous ring closures and an oxidation, is converted to lanosterol, a compound closely related to cholesterol. Lanosterol is readily transformed into cholesterol (Chap. IV, Sect. I-5).

This research illustrates the methods used for "sequence analysis": suppose you wish to prove that compound B is on the pathway between A and C, thus: A → B → C. First, feed radioactive A and observe the appearance of label in C (experiment 1). Then feed labeled A together with unlabeled B, and again observe the label in C (experiment 2). If B is truly on the pathway, the small amount of radioactive B normally formed from labeled A will be diluted by the large amount of administered unlabeled B. There will be two consequences: (*a*) because of the dilution of the labeled B by unlabeled B, the radioactivity in C will drop, compared to that seen in experiment 1; (*b*) compound B can be re-isolated and, if truly on the pathway, will now be itself radioactive. To clinch the argument, one then takes the labeled B and feeds it in place of labeled A (experiment 3). Again, compound C should be labeled.

5. BIOSYNTHESIS OF VALINE

Methods of this sort have been used to map metabolic pathways in the synthesis of fatty acids, sugars, purines, pyrimidines, and amino acids. A particularly interesting experiment, by Strassman and Weinhouse, revealed the metabolic pathway for the synthesis of the amino acid valine in microorganisms. All carbon atoms of valine are derived from pyruvate. On degradation of valine, the distribution of radioactivity was as shown in Table IV.

TABLE IV

DISTRIBUTION OF RADIOACTIVITY IN VALINE FROM LABELED PYRUVATE IN MICROORGANISMS[a]

Valine		Valine C atom	Label (%) in valine from pyruvate labeled in		
			CH_3	CO	COOH
COOH	1	1	1	3	99
CHNH₂	2	2	4	49	0
CH	3	3	4	47	1
CH₃ CH₃	4,4'	4,4'	91	1	0

[a] From Strassman and Weinhouse (1955).

Table IV shows that the methyl group of pyruvate provided the methyl groups of valine (4 and 4'); the carboxyl group of pyruvate, the carboxyl group of valine (1). But how can the middle carbon atom of pyruvate label *both* the middle carbon atoms (2 and 3) of valine? An ingenious pathway was suggested, since confirmed by other experiments:

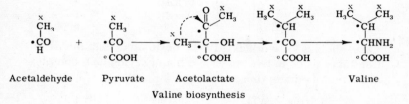

| Acetaldehyde | Pyruvate | Acetolactate | | Valine |

Valine biosynthesis

Pyruvate is known to lose its carboxyl group to give acetaldehyde, which condenses with another molecule of pyruvate to give acetolactic acid. This reaction is known to take place in bacteria. Now, to produce the valine skeleton from this compound, one methyl group must move from carbon 2 to carbon 3, as shown. This reaction is familiar to organic chemists ("pinacole rearrangement"). It completely accounts for the distribution of radioactivity in valine. It is an extraordinary biochemical reaction: the migration of a methyl group from one carbon in a molecule to another, in the course of the biosynthesis of an amino acid. It could have been detected only by isotope incorporation and analysis of isotope distribution in the product from a single precursor, labeled in three different positions.

6. Enzyme-Substrate Complex as an Intermediate

A powerful tool for the investigation of the mechanisms of enzymatic reactions is the incorporation of labeled molecules into unlabeled compounds in reversible enzymatic reactions. A good example is the carboxylation of propionic acid (activated as the coenzyme A derivative, propionyl-CoA) with carbon dioxide (CO_2) to produce methylmalonic acid (as the coenzyme A derivative, methylmalonyl-CoA), a reaction catalyzed by the enzyme "propionyl carboxylase" and requiring adenosine triphosphate (ATP) as an energy source:

(1) CH_3CH_2CO—CoA + ATP + CO_2 $\overset{\text{enzyme}}{\rightleftharpoons}$
Propionyl-CoA

$\qquad\qquad\qquad CH_3CHCO$—CoA   + ADP + P_i

$\qquad\qquad\qquad\qquad\diagdown COOH$

$\qquad\qquad$Methylmalonyl-CoA   Inorganic
$\qquad\qquad\qquad\qquad\qquad\qquad\qquad\qquad\qquad$phosphate

Lane and his co-workers (1960) postulated that this reaction takes place in two stages, with an enzyme-CO_2 complex as an intermediate, thus:

(2)   Enzyme + ATP + CO_2 $\rightleftharpoons$ enzyme-CO_2 + ADP + P_i

(3) Enzyme-CO_2 + propionyl-CoA $\rightleftharpoons$ methylmalonyl-CoA + enzyme

Take C^{14}-propionyl-CoA and the enzyme, incubate them together: nothing happens, since CO_2 and ATP are missing (see reaction 1, above). Now, incubate C^{14}-propionyl-CoA with *unlabeled* methylmalonyl-CoA and enzyme, then re-isolate the methylmalonyl-CoA: it is now radioactive. How could this have happened, when propionyl-CoA and enzyme do not react? The explanation is this: the unlabeled methyl-malonyl-CoA and enzyme form unlabeled propionyl-CoA and enzyme-CO_2 complex (reversal of reaction 3, above). The enzyme-CO_2 complex now reacts with some of the *labeled* propionyl-CoA in the mixture, to give *labeled* methylmalonyl-CoA (reaction 3). These results cannot be explained without the assumption of the enzyme-CO_2 complex; they are therefore proof of the existence of such a complex between enzyme and substrate, and of the occurrence of reaction 3.

To give the reader an idea of the actual experiment: 0.26 micromole of propionyl-CoA containing 273×10^3 c.p.m. was incubated in buffer solution at 37°C with methylmal-onyl-CoA (0.55 micromole), enzyme (0.06 mg.), and magnesium chloride (4 micromoles). The reaction was stopped after 30 minutes by heating to 100°C, and the methyl-malonyl-CoA was isolated by paper chromatography. It now had 17×10^3 c.p.m. of radioactivity.

The principle of the isotope incorporation in absence of net synthesis can also be applied to a study of the mechanism of irreversible enzymatic reactions (Peterkofsky, 1962). Histidine is irreversibly changed to urocanic acid and ammonia by the enzyme histidase:

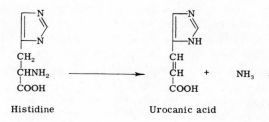

Histidine   Urocanic acid

If the enzyme is incubated with NH_3 and C^{14}-urocanic acid, no histidine appears, because the reaction is not reversible. However, if C^{14}-urocanic acid is incubated with the enzyme and *unlabeled* histidine, the histidine becomes labeled in the course of the incubation.

This could happen only if an enzyme-NH_3 complex is postulated as an intermediate:

(*1*)   Enzyme + histidine $\leftrightharpoons$ urocanic acid + enzyme-NH_3

(*2*)   Enzyme-NH_3 → enzyme + NH_3

C^{14}-urocanic acid and NH_3, when incubated with the enzyme, cannot combine, because the enzyme-NH_3 complex is lacking. This cannot be formed from enzyme plus NH_3, because reaction 2, above, is irreversible. However, if C^{14}-urocanic acid is incubated with unlabeled histidine and enzyme, the histidine is first spit into urocanic acid and enzyme-NH_3 complex (reaction 1). *This complex* can now react with the *labeled* urocanic acid to produce labeled histidine (reverse reaction 1). The experiment suggests the existence of the enzyme-NH_3 complex.

B. Protein Synthesis and the Transfer of Genetic Information

The main lines and many of the details of the metabolic pathways of the small molecular-weight compounds were laid down by the 1950's. The stage was set for what may become known as the great achievement in biology of the 1960's: the exploration of the biological macromolecules. Here resided the last trace of a belief in "vitalism," the idea that something special and different imbues living things, which is not amenable to analysis by chemistry and physics.

Living matter depends entirely on the workings of enzymes. They act together in finely coordinated teams, and make possible the highly organized flow of chemical reactions that we call "life." Now, enzyme reactions can be made to work in the test tube, even in coordinated teams of enzymes. But the question *"How are the enzymes themselves made?"* has been until recently the last resort of the vitalist. We know that ultimately the genetic control, in other words, the constancy of a species of organism, is made effective through control of enzyme synthesis. In one species, the same enzymes are made, from generation to generation, assuring the same chemical reactions, and therefore the constancy of the species. A mutation is a change in the pattern of enzyme synthesis. But, *"How is enzyme synthesis controlled?"* This has been the second vitalist mystery.

The answers to these questions, in terms of known chemical reactions, have been given by the new science of molecular biology. Progress has been amazingly rapid, and any lingering feelings of "vitalism" have disappeared. The enzymes are proteins, and the genetic control exerted on their synthesis is through a chemical compound, deoxyribonucleic acid (DNA). Both these classes of material are macromolecules, i.e., the molecules are huge, of molecular weight in the hundred thousand or million range. It was here, in the investigation of the synthesis of the macromolecules, that isotopes have made so large a contribution.

7. PROTEIN SYNTHESIS

As long ago as 1953, Spiegelman discovered that enzymes are synthesized not from other proteins, but from free amino acids. This important fact, which lies at the basis of our knowledge of protein biosynthesis, was established by a neat isotope experiment.

A strain of bacteria (*Escherichia coli*) was grown in a medium with uniformly C^{14}-labeled lactic acid as the only carbon source. In other words, the only carbon the bacteria obtained was labeled with C^{14}, so that *all* carbon atoms, including of course those of the proteins, were labeled. These radioactive bacteria were then made to synthesize one particular enzyme, which they did not have before (an "induced" enzyme), at the same time that they were given unlabeled amino acids to feed on in their medium. The new enzyme was isolated and purified. It contained practically no label. Therefore, the enzyme must have been made from the unlabeled free amino acids, put into the medium at the same moment as the enzyme inducer, rather than from the labeled protein already in the bacterial cells.

Subsequently, the whole enzymatic machine that makes protein from amino acids was pulled out of the cell, taken apart into its components: ribonucleic acids (RNA's), enzymes, energy-yielding substrate (ATP), cofactors, and the substrates (amino acids); and then put together again in the test tube to make protein (Zamecnick, 1960). The mechanism of the synthesis was studied; however, as discussed for the case of cholesterol biosynthesis, net synthesis was so minutely small, that it could be detected only by incorporation of radioactive amino acids.

Amino acids first combine with ATP for "activation," i.e., to bring them to an energy level adequate for the subsequent reactions. They are then attached to the ends of the molecules of a specific ribonucleic acid, RNA (s for "soluble"), of relatively small molecular weight (about 2.5×10^4). There is a specific s-RNA for every amino acid, which can recognize the amino acid and pick it up (with the aid of an enzyme), so as to carry it to the site of protein synthesis. This synthesis takes place on a kind of RNA in the form of a particle, the ribosome. All these facts were gathered by taking the components of the protein synthesizing system mentioned, from animal or bacterial cells, and letting the enzymes, RNA's, etc. react with the radioactive amino acids. Protein was isolated at the end of the reaction. The amount of radioactivity incorporated was a measure of the extent of protein synthesis. However, a new factor intervened, which required new techniques beyond simple radioactivity incorporation.

8. THE NUCLEIC ACIDS AND PROTEIN SYNTHESIS

As was discussed in the chapter on autoradiography (Chap. V, Sect. II-4), the whole genetic information of every cell resides in the chromosomes in a special type of nucleic acid, deoxyribonucleic acid (DNA). When a new cell is born, it receives from the parent all the "instructions" it needs to live and, what is more, to live in a way identical to the parent, in the form of a copy of the parent's own DNA. But how does the daughter cell convert the information it receives, in the form of a strand of DNA, into the organized cell material which is what we mean by "living" substance? All the things that the cell has and does are made by enzymes. Enzymes are proteins ordered in a very definite, specific way. Therefore, the DNA strand has to *direct*, in some way, the synthesis of proteins. We have just learned that proteins are synthesized on the ribosomes. How does the DNA of the cell influence the synthesis of proteins on the ribosome?

Both RNA and DNA are long chains of purine and

pyrimidine molecules, held together by links through phosphate and ribose or deoxyribose (Fig. 6). The sequence in which the purines and pyrimidines are arranged in the chain determines or directs the sequence of amino acids joined together to make a protein on the ribosome. And, of course, it is the *sequence* of amino acids that gives each protein molecule its specific enzymatic properties, its ability to catalyze some reaction in the cell. Rich (1962) states, "Sequence is equivalent to information, just as the sequence of letters of the alphabet conveys information." The great hypothesis that set the stage for the recent advance in knowledge of biology on the molecular level, was derived by Watson and Crick (cf. Chap. V, Sect. II-4). This states that DNA is not a single but a double-stranded chain. The two strands are linked in such a way that to each particular pyrimidine in one chain, there is joined (by weak links) a particular purine in the other, and to each purine in one chain, a pyrimidine in the other. In chemical terms, the strands are held together by hydrogen bonds between complementary pairs of bases (purines and pyrimidines are bases). To replicate, the strands separate and each builds up its partner again by assembling the matching purine or pyrimidine molecule along its length ("base pairing"). Now, protein synthesis occurs not on the DNA of the chromosomes in the cell nucleus, but on the ribosome particles in the cytoplasm. Therefore, to direct protein synthesis, the information must be transferred from the DNA to a "messenger" which is sent out of the nucleus to the site of protein synthesis. To do this, a strand of DNA builds up along its length a molecule of RNA, by base pairing, for each purine a matching pyrimidine. This RNA molecule is now a "negative" copy of the DNA. It becomes detached from the DNA and is sent out of the cell nucleus to the site of protein synthesis, carrying with it the information coded in the DNA. At first, it was thought that the ribosomal RNA is the code copy of the DNA. However, ribosomal RNA was found to differ completely in base composition from DNA: if it were the "messenger," its base composition would have to match exactly that of the DNA. At this stage some isotope experiments were done to decide the question. These experiments merit detailed description as models of ingenuity, and to demonstrate what can be achieved by the isotope technique in molecular biology.

9. MESSENGER RNA

Bacterial cells can be infected by a type of virus called bacteriophage (type T-2). The virus (or T-2, for short) consists essentially of nothing else but DNA (T-2 DNA). When the bacterial cell (*E. coli*) is injected with this bacteriophage, the latter multiplies inside the bacterial cell, using the substance of the bacteria as raw material for growth. This is really what is meant by "infection." However, to multiply, that is, to replicate the T-2 DNA, the virus needs enzymes. Their synthesis must, of course, be directed by the T-2 DNA. This it does by first making T-2 RNA. This RNA is the "messenger" which, with bacterial amino acids, and on the bacterial ribosomes, makes the T-2 enzymes. The purine and pyrimidine base composition of the T-2 RNA (i.e., the RNA synthesized within the bacterial cell after infection by T-2) exactly matches that of the T-2 DNA, not the bacterial RNA. Here we have a system, therefore, where one particular RNA and one particular kind of protein only are being synthesized.

Brenner *et al.* (1961; and earlier, Meselson and Stahl, 1958) used isotopes, not simply as markers to identify some particular molecule among a large crowd of other unmarked molecules, but to impart to certain substances greater molecular weight, so that they would behave differently on centrifugation. They grew bacterial cells in the presence simultaneously of C^{13}-labeled amino acids and N^{15}-labeled ammonium chloride. In consequence, the bacteria grew up with almost all their carbon and nitrogen in the form of heavy atoms (C^{13} instead of C^{12}, N^{15} instead of N^{14}), though not, of course, radioactive (C^{13} and N^{15} are stable isotopes). The "heavy" bacteria were then infected with T-2 virus, and immediately transferred to a normal, unlabeled ("light") medium, which contained a small amount of *radioactive* intermediates (C^{14}-uracil or P^{32}-phosphate). These compounds specifically label RNA. Therefore, all constituents newly synthesized after T-2 infection would be "light," and the RNA synthesized after infection would be radioactive.

All the different kinds of RNA, old bacterial (i.e., from before infection), ribosomal, and new T-2 RNA, were then isolated and separated by "density gradient centrifugation." This means that the mixture of RNA's is placed in a centrifuge tube containing caesium chloride solution. When this solution is centrifuged at very high speed (about $100,000 \times$ gravity) for several days, the caesium chloride forms itself into layers of increasing density. The molecules of RNA dissolved in it then become distributed in this density gradient at particular layers corresponding to their own density, which differs for different molecular species. In this way, the C^{13}-N^{15} RNA, the normal (C^{12}-N^{14}) RNA, and the small T-2 RNA (labeled with radioactivity) could be separated. In other words, stable isotopes are here used to impart greater density and molecular weight to compounds in order that they can be *separated* by centrifugation from identical, nonisotopic molecules. This use of isotopes for purposes of separation rather than detection is new and unprecedented.

It was found upon centrifugation that the new, radioactive RNA was attached to old ("heavy") ribosomes, but could be released by treatment with a solution of low magnesium concentration. This RNA, being radioactive, must, of course, have been made after infection. It is not detectable other than by the radioactivity it contains. Its purine and pyrimidine base composition matched that of

T-2 DNA, not that of bacterial RNA. What this experiment revealed, therefore, is that the virus DNA, after it enters the cell, begins to make its own RNA (the "messenger"), which becomes attached to existing bacterial ribosomes, in order there presumably to make new protein, as directed by the virus DNA (since it contained the virus DNA code, i.e., base composition).

That new protein was being made could be shown by exposing the bacterial cells briefly to S^{35}-labeled amino acids in their growth medium, after T-2 infection. Since sulfur occurs only in protein and not in RNA or DNA, any labeling by radioactive sulfur amongst the macromolecules must be on account of protein synthesis. Upon density gradient centrifugation, the S^{35} label was found at the same place as the m-RNA (m for "messenger"): the old or "heavy" RNA of the bacterial ribosomes. If the short exposure to S^{35}-labeled amino acids (short "pulse") was followed by a period in which the infected bacteria were fed ordinary, unlabeled sulfur (S^{32}; an S^{32} "chaser"), then the S^{35}-protein appeared no longer attached to the old bacterial ribosomes, but amongst the proteins of the bacterial cell. This means that, as soon as the virus starts its own m-RNA synthesis in the bacterial cell, protein is also made, at the same spot where the m-RNA is found (the bacterial ribosome). When completed, the new protein is detached and sent to its proper functional place in the cell.

10. NUCLEIC ACID HYBRIDIZATION

Very cogent evidence for the existence of the messenger-RNA was obtained by Hall and Spiegelman (1961). The hypothesis is the following: when the T-2 virus infects an *E. coli* cell, some of the T-2 DNA separates and from a double strand forms two single ones. Along one of these single strands the new T-2 RNA (the "messenger") has to be assembled. When the assembly is complete, it becomes detached and starts T-2 protein synthesis, using the bacterial protein synthesis machine, including the bacterial ribosomes, together with T-2 "information."

It is possible, artificially, to make single-stranded DNA, by heating ordinary, double-stranded DNA to a specific temperature, followed by fast cooling ("heat-denatured DNA"). When this is put into solution together with T-2 RNA and heated and cooled, a double-stranded DNA-RNA hybrid can be made, provided the purine and pyrimidine bases of the DNA and RNA are complementary. Spiegelman and his group made denatured, single-stranded T-2 DNA labeled with tritium, by growing the virus in presence of tritium-labeled thymidine, followed by heat denaturation. They then prepared some T-2 RNA labeled with P^{32}, by infecting bacterial cells with virus in presence of radioactive phosphate. Since the only RNA synthesized after infection is T-2 RNA, a pure sample of P^{32}-labeled T-2 RNA was thus obtained. The denatured, tritium-labeled T-2 DNA and the P^{32}-labeled T-2 RNA were heated and cooled together, and centrifuged. There appeared, of course, bands of tritium alone (DNA), and of P^{32} alone (RNA). But also, a single band was isolated, containing tritium and P^{32} together—clear proof of hybrid formation between the DNA and RNA. No such hybrid was formed from undenatured DNA. If, instead of DNA from the T-2 virus, that of another species of virus (T-5) was used, no hybrid could be obtained with T-2 RNA. Hybrid formation is proof of base complementarity. Therefore, the T-2 RNA formed after infection has bases to match those of the T-2 DNA only, and no other species of virus or bacteria. In other words, it carries the T-2 information or "message" to the site of protein synthesis.

Spiegelman and his team later, demonstrated that the DNA-RNA hybrid occurs naturally, as indeed it must, if at some stage the DNA code is imparted to the RNA. Spiegelman did this by growing his virus in P^{32}-phosphate, thus making radioactive, P^{32}-labeled T-2 DNA. He then infected bacteria with this virus, at the same time adding tritium-labeled uridine. This base is specifically taken up by RNA. Tritium-labeled m-RNA would therefore result. The nucleic acids were separated by density gradient centrifugation: a P^{32}-labeled DNA band appeared, a tritium-labeled m-RNA band, and a band in a position corresponding to the molecular weight of a DNA-RNA hybrid, having in it both the P^{32} and tritium labels. This hybrid must have been formed, not as in the previous experiment by artificially making single-stranded DNA and causing it to combine with m-RNA, but in the natural course of m-RNA synthesis. The T-2 DNA must have separated, and the m-RNA been laid down along a single strand, as predicted by the Watson-Crick hypothesis.

Pure messenger RNA can now be isolated and, together with the components of the protein synthesizing machinery, will make specific proteins. It is of the greatest importance to note that the protein-synthesizing enzymes, and the ribosomes, can be of one species (e.g., bacteria), and the m-RNA of another (e.g., virus): the protein produced (since the base sequence in m-RNA is genetically determined by the DNA of its own species) will be of the species which provides the m-RNA.

It has recently even been possible to synthesize m-RNA in the test tube for which process, as might be expected, some DNA had to be present. The m-RNA was built onto this DNA, in presence of the purine and pyrimidine bases (as the ribose triphosphates) as raw material, and the enzyme RNA polymerase. Its base composition was, of course, complementary to that of the DNA used as "template."

11. TURNOVER OF M-RNA

The experiments of Brenner (Chap. VI, Sect. II-9) indicated that ribosomal RNA is long-lived, whereas m-RNA has a short life, that is, a rapid turnover. This is what one would expect: to make new and different protein molecules every moment, with information transferred from different portions of the chromosome, the m-RNA would have to be destroyed quite soon after it is formed. The question of the length of life of a molecule of m-RNA was neatly answered in a pulse-labeling experiment by Levinthal *et al.* (1962). They used the antibiotic actinomycin D, which becomes attached to DNA and thus prevents further synthesis of m-RNA. A growing culture of the bacterium *Bacillus subtilis* was exposed to a 30-second pulse of C^{14}-uracil, then actinomycin was added. During exposure to the pulse, a small amount of m-RNA was made by the cells, labeled with C^{14}. The antibiotic stopped further m-RNA synthesis. The m-RNA was then isolated (detectable as a radioactive band only, on centrifugation, as the quantity would be much too small to be visible spectrophotometrically), at different times after actinomycin addition. Since the antibiotic prevented the production of more m-RNA, the existing radioactive m-RNA disappeared rapidly, as it was being destroyed and broken down into its constituent bases, without being repleted. The disappearance rate followed an exponential curve. From this curve it was calculated that the life of a molecule of m-RNA is about 2 minutes. From the assumption that three bases iń the RNA determine the positioning in the protein sequence of one amino acid ("triplet code"), and from the knowledge of the amount of protein made in the lifetime of a m-RNA molecule (2 minutes), it was possible to calculate that each messenger makes 10–20 molecules of protein, and that it therefore requires 5–10 seconds to make one protein molecule.

12. Assembly of Amino Acids

Are the amino acids first assembled on the m-RNA-ribosome complex and then all simultaneously zipped together to make the protein, or is the protein made gradually, by sequential addition of amino acids to a steadily growing chain? This question was unequivocally answered in an ingenious and classical experiment by Dintzis (1961). It was first necessary to find a cell which produced only one type of protein. The immature red blood cell (reticulocyte) is such a cell since, on incubation in the right medium, it forms only hemoglobin (Hb), and continues to do so for several hours. Any living reticulocyte contains 10–20% by weight of finished Hb and, attached to the reticulocyte ribosome, unfinished Hb at various stages of development. Both the finished and the unfinished Hb can be subjected to enzymatic digestion, for instance with trypsin, which breaks the complete chains (or the incomplete ones on the ribosomes) into pieces at definite sites. These pieces ("peptides") can be definitely recognized and identified, after they are separated by paper chromatography. If the reticulocyte is given a radioactive amino acid in the incubation medium at a given moment, for a long or a short time (pulse), then the protein formed after that moment will be radioactive. Consider the hypothesis that the protein chain is initiated at one end and built up in sequence, by addition of one amino acid after another to the end. If it is then digested, it will give peptides *a, b, c* at the beginning, and end with *e, f, g*. Suppose now, one gives the cell a *short* pulse of radioactive amino acid: then the completed Hb molecules isolated would have only a few peptides labeled, and these would be only *g*, or *f* and *g* or *e, f*, and *g*, but not *a, b*, or *c* (Fig. 4B). If one were to plot radioactivity against peptide (Fig. 5), the curve would show a steep gradient (x—x). After a *long* pulse, the completed Hb molecules would have label in more peptides, resulting in a shallow gradient of the radioactivity-peptide curve (●—●). When exposed for a very long time (1 hour) to a radioactive amino acid, every peptide would be labeled; the "curve" would be horizontal (+—+; ■—■). But always one peptide, the end peptide, *g*, will have the highest radioactivity. Another, the initiating peptide, *a*, the lowest radioactivity. So much for those Hb molecules that are completed and found in solution within the cell.

The situation would be quite different for the partly finished chains still on the ribosomes. Here a *short* pulse would result in labeling of all the short peptide chains in process of formation—each growing, unlabeled chain would have a small, labeled peptide added to its end. On the other hand, after a *long* pulse, all peptides near the starting point, *a*, *ab*, *abc*, etc., would be labeled, but the longer peptides which had already begun to be laid down before the pulse, *abc . . . e*, *abc . . . ef*, *abc . . . efg*, would have long stretches of nonradioactive peptides. Since there are more peptides at any moment that contain *a* than those that contain *b*, more of those that contain *b* than *c*, etc. (Fig. 4A), the gradient would be the reverse of that expected for the finished Hb: it would be shallow for the short pulse and steep for the long pulse. So peptide *a*, as it occurs most frequently in the growing peptide which all molecules start with, would be the most radioactive, and there would be fewest peptides having radioactive *g*. In the actual experiment, an internal base line for radioactivity measurements had to be obtained, which automatically corrected for losses and unequal amino acid composition of the peptides. This was done by a very long pulse. The reticulocytes were exposed to the C-14-labeled amino acid leucine for 5 hours, until every leucine in every peptide was labeled. Now the pulses, long or short, were made with H^3-leucine, and the incorporation expressed not as absolute radioactivity incorporation, but as H^3/C^{14} ratio, which represented a *corrected* measure of incorporation. Under the conditions of the experiment, 35 peptides were obtained, numbered 1 to 35. Numbers 27 and 16 were the highest labeled from the soluble, completed Hb (*f* and *g*); others were lower, the gradients being shown in Fig. 5 for pulses of different duration. The gradient was steep for the 7-

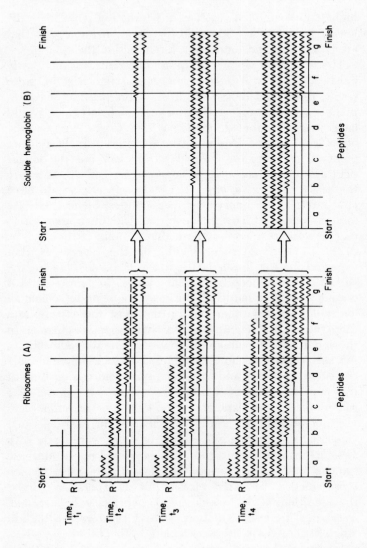

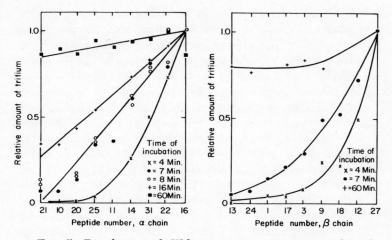

FIG. 5. Distribution of H³-leucine among tryptic peptides of soluble rabbit hemoglobin after various times of incubation at 15°C. [From H. M. Dintzis, *Proc. Natl. Sci. U. S.* **47**, 247 (1961).]

minute, shallow for the 16-minute pulse. The ribosomal fragments, on the other hand, from which the same 35 peptides were obtained, showed least radioactivity in peptides 27 and 16. Here the gradients were the reverse: shallow in

---

FIG. 4. Model of sequential chain growth. The straight lines represent unlabeled polypeptide chain. The zigzag lines represent radioactively labeled polypeptide chain formed after the addition of radioactive amino acid at time t_1. The groups of peptides labeled R are those unfinished bits attached to the ribosomes at each time; the rest, having reached the finish line, are assumed to be present in the soluble hemoglobin. In the ribosome at time t_2, the top two completely zigzag lines represent peptide chains formed completely from amino acids during the time interval between t_1 and t_2. The middle two lines represent chains which have grown during the time interval but have not reached the finish line and are therefore still attached to the ribosomes. The bottom two chains represent those which have crossed the finish line, left the ribosomes, and are to be found mixed with other molecules of soluble hemoglobin. [From H. M. Dintzis, *U. S. Proc. Natl. Acad. Sci.* **47**, 247 (1961).]

the 7-minute pulse, steep in the 16-minute pulse. The experiment completely agreed, therefore, with the prediction for a stepwise addition of amino acids to the chain. Now, every protein, being a chain of amino acids, has an amino ($—NH_2$) and a carboxyl ($—COOH$) end. Dintzis showed that the end peptide (number 16, g), which in the completed Hb has the highest radioactivity, when treated with a special enzyme specific for carboxyl ends of proteins, could be split off. It can therefore be concluded that the protein Hb is made sequentially, starting from an amino end and ending with a carboxyl end. From the time it took to label the molecule, one could calculate that about two amino acids per second were added onto the chain.

This experiment shows that a huge amount of the most basic knowledge of biological processes can be extracted from a single superbly conceived and relatively simple experiment.

13. THE TRANSLATION MECHANISM: RNA TO PROTEIN

As Spiegelman has pointed out, the genetic language of the DNA is merely *transcribed* into the almost identical language of the RNA. But it ultimately has to be *translated* into the quite different language of the protein. The "dictionary" which enables the cell to translate the four-word (2 purine, 2 pyrimidine bases) into the 20-word (20 amino acids) language, is the soluble RNA (s-RNA) already mentioned (Chap. VI, Sect. II-7). For this RNA combines with amino acids, and carries them to the m-RNA-ribosome complex, where they are assembled to form protein. The sequence in which they are put together is, of course, determined by the m-RNA which is situated on the ribosome. There is a different and specific s-RNA for each amino acid. Therefore, one must conclude that the m-RNA can "recognize" each one of the 20 different s-RNA molecules with their particular amino acid, in order to assemble them correctly. The "recognition," of course, is again the process of base pairing. Suppose the next amino acid in the sequence of protein at this moment is to be glycine: the messenger RNA will have 3 bases (say, a pyrilidine and 2 purines) which match 3 complementary bases (a purine and 2 pyrilidines) on the s-RNA carrying glycine. This s-RNA will move up and combine with the m-RNA and thus put glycine in its place in the amino acid sequence. The translation of the nucleic acid into the protein language is complete.

It is remarkable that, in the course of evolution, the "languages" of the nucleic acids and proteins have not changed; they are "universal languages." Take rabbit m-RNA, which instructs the protein-synthesizing machine to make, say, hemoglobin (von Ehrenstein and Lipmann, 1961). Now, rabbit hemoglobin will be made, whether one uses the s-RNA of the rabbit to pick up the amino acids and assemble them on the m-RNA-ribosome complex, or whether one were to use s-RNA of bacteria. The *instruction* comes from the m-RNA. The s-RNA of rabbit or bacteria, or presumably any other species, can understand this instruction and carry it out by the mechanism of base pairing. Thus, von Ehrenstein and Lipmann incubated s-RNA from *E. coli* with C^{14}-leucine attached to it (as well as all the other amino acids in nonradioactive form) with rabbit reticulocyte ribosomes (presumed to be carrying the correct m-RNA for hemoglobin synthesis). To make sure that only C^{14}-leucyl-s-RNA was incorporated, and not leucine in the free state or attached to any other RNA present, the investigators added free nonradioactive leucine to the incubation mixture, which would instantly and greatly dilute the radioactivity of any free leucine that might be present.

Carrier hemoglobin was added at the end of the incubation time, and the hemoglobin isolated by column chromatography. A radioactive peak was eluted, corresponding exactly to the peak for carrier hemoglobin, thus proving that bacterial s-RNA can carry amino acids into rabbit hemoglobin.

Though the s-RNA is not species-specific, and can translate into protein whatever message it receives from m-RNA, it still must itself be made on instruction, ultimately from DNA. Giacomoni and Spiegelman (1962) demonstrated that, whereas long stretches of DNA are complementary to m-RNA, and thus transfer large amounts of DNA information, there are small stretches on the DNA which are complementary to s-RNA. In other words, the s-RNA is also built up by complementary base pairing along a *small* part of the DNA. In order to demonstrate this, they used the hybrid formation between DNA and RNA, which is proof of base complementarity (Chap. VI, Sect. II-10). However, since only a minute proportion of the DNA was hybridized with s-RNA, it was necessary to employ enormously high radioactivity in the s-RNA (e.g., 200,000 c.p.m. per microgram of P^{32}) to detect the hybrid. Heat-denatured (i.e., single-stranded) DNA from *E. coli* was incubated with P^{32}-labeled s-RNA from *E. coli*, and tritium-labeled s-RNA from *Bacillus megatherium*. Density gradient centrifugation followed, in which a band of DNA (recognizable by its ultraviolet light absorption spectrum) also contained radioactivity from the P^{32} of the *E. coli* s-RNA. The *quantity* of this s-RNA hybridized was of course minute; when the DNA was saturated by s-RNA, it represented only 0.02% of the DNA. In other words, 0.02% of the DNA sequence of *E. coli* is coded to make s-RNA. The proportion of DNA coding for *m-RNA* can be as high as 100%.

The DNA band contained no tritium label. Therefore, *E. coli* DNA codes for *E. coli* s-RNA but not for s-RNA of *B. megatherium*, since the latter carried the tritium label. Conversely, the tritium-labeled *B. megatherium* s-RNA coincided with a band of *B. megatherium* DNA, but not with

Pseudomonas DNA, in an appropriate experiment. Therefore, each species makes its own s-RNA, following the base
sequence in a short stretch of its DNA. This does not
mean, of course, that s-RNA is species-specific in its function of aligning amino acids on m-RNA ribosomes. This
function is universal and depends on a universal occurrence of one base sequence coding for each amino acid. The
rest of s-RNA, outside of the three bases which recognize
the particular amino acid, is coded specifically by the DNA
of each species.

14. DNA SYNTHESIS

Of the two fundamental and universal life processes,
one, the making of enzymes under genetic control, has been
described above, at least in outline. Some aspects of the
second, the reproduction of the genetic substance itself,
will now be discussed.

How does the genetic substance, DNA, make copies of
itself? The answer was found by Kornberg (1961) and his
co-workers in what must be described as the triumph of
molecular biology: an enzyme which, through a series of
definite, known chemical reactions, can, in the test tube,
cause the synthesis of DNA and thereby the genetic code
which directs all activities of the cell. In the words of
Kornberg, "When a parent cell is to divide, this chemical
code must be duplicated or replicated perfectly so that the
daughter cells will have a complete set of instructions for
their own complex development and that of countless future generations of their progeny. DNA must be regarded
not only as the blueprint but also as the mold. It provides
the link from one cell generation to the next and also
serves as the original template for the manufacture of the
cell's structural proteins and its enzymatic machinery, which
will determine every detail of its appearance and intricate
behavior."

Again, the theory of Watson and Crick (cf. Chap. VI,

Sect. II-8) was the basis for the proposed mechanism of replication: that the material of the genes, the DNA, consists of two strands, held together by weak bonds ("hydrogen bonds") between complementary pairs of bases, each particular purine to a particular pyrimidine. The theory then stated that, in order to replicate, the strands separate and a new strand of DNA is laid down along each of the two existing strands, by pairing of complementary bases. When finished, there would be two pairs where there had been one before, each new pair consisting of a strand of the old DNA linked to a strand of new DNA. This molecular model of the behavior of chromosomes in cell division is, of course, in complete accord with the knowledge of genetics accumulated over the last hundred years, beginning with Mendel. It has been visually confirmed in the experiments of Taylor (Chap. V, Sect. II-4) by autoradiography.

Kornberg extracted an enzyme ("DNA polymerase") from bacteria, and placed it in a test tube, together with a mixture of the four bases (in the form of their sugar-phosphate derivatives, i.e., deoxyribose triphosphates) in solution: nothing happened. But if the enzyme and bases were incubated with a very small amount of fully made and complete DNA ("primer"), more DNA was synthesized. The enormous power of the radioactive isotope incorporation method is here illustrated. DNA synthesis was measured by making one of the bases (thymidine) radioactive, and assaying for radioactivity in the DNA at the end of the reaction. As Kornberg states, in the first experiments, before the enzyme had been purified, the net synthesis of DNA was 10 micromicromoles (one micromicromole of thymidine is 242×10^{-11} gram or 24 ten-billionths of a gram), or 1/10,000 of the amount that can be measured by the most sensitive chemical methods. This was 50 c.p.m. in the DNA isolated upon incubation of 5 million c.p.m. of C^{14}-thymidine. Guided by this assay, purification of the enzyme was achieved, until sufficient DNA could be synthesized for chemical as well as radiochemical determination of net synthesis. An analysis of the bases in the newly synthesized DNA revealed a composition which showed base complementarity to the primer that had to be used to start the reaction. This is as one would have predicted from the Watson-Crick postulate: a very small amount of complete DNA must be there so that the new bases can be laid down along the length of the complete strand to form the new molecule. More strands are made with the newly formed DNA. The rate of the synthesis becomes greater and greater as more DNA is made and is available as template for still more. Theoretically, all the system would need is one molecule of primer DNA to spark it off. In actual experiments, the DNA made by the enzyme was about 20 times that added as primer. As stated by Kornberg (1961), "The enzyme is unique in that it takes directions from a template."

15. "NEAREST NEIGHBOR" ANALYSIS

So far the over-all base composition of the synthetic DNA showed complementarity to that of the primer. But if the DNA is the "genetic code" that directs protein synthesis, then it must be the *sequence* of bases that has to be replicated when DNA is synthesized. Kornberg devised an isotopic method for discovering, not the complete sequence, but at least the next neighboring base for each base ("nearest neighbor" sequence). Suppose you had base Y (Fig. 6), with the sugar deoxyribose and labeled phosphate (P^{32}), which is linked to position 5 of the sugar. During synthesis, catalyzed by DNA polymerase, the labeled phosphate group (P^{*}) becomes linked to sugar-position 3 of the end group of the DNA strand already made (the "growing end"). Thus, labeled phosphorus links the bases X and Y through the 3 and 5 positions of the sugars. After the completed, P^{32}-labeled DNA (about 10^{16} such bonds are formed) is isolated, it is enzymatically digested. Enzymes are used which split the phosphate-sugar link at position 5 of DNA. Therefore, whereas radioactive phosphate was attached to base Y before synthesis, it is now, after degradation, found to be on base X (see Fig. 6).

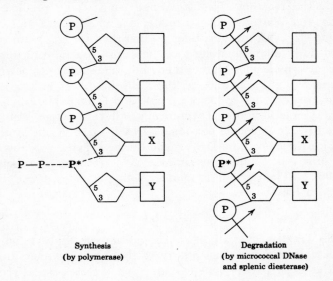

Synthesis
(by polymerase)

Degradation
(by micrococcal DNase
and splenic diesterase)

Fig. 6. Synthesis of a P³²-labeled DNA chain and its subsequent enzymatic degradation to 3′-deoxyribonucleotides. The arrows indicate the linkages cleaved by microccal DNase and calf-spleen phosphodiesterase, yielding a digest composed exclusively of 3′-deoxyribonucleotides. *Rectangles,* purine and pyrimidine bases. *Pentagons,* deoxyribose (sugars). *Circles,* phosphate groups. [From A. Kornberg, "Enzymatic Syntheses of DNA." Wiley, New York, 1961.]

Therefore, X must have been the nearest neighbor of Y. The amount of radioactivity in X is then a measure of the relative frequency with which X neighbors Y in the synthetic DNA. Since there are four bases that make up the sequence (call them A, C, T, G), four separate incubations are done, with P³² on A, on C, on T, and on G. After isolation and enzymatic digestion of the DNA synthesized, the *neighbors* of A, of C, of T, and of G are found to be labeled. This experiment, first of all, provided a new way of checking base complementarity between the primer DNA and the synthetic DNA: the so-called base ratio, that is, the ratio of all the radioactivity in A plus T to that in G plus C, was the same as the *chemically* determined A plus T to G plus C ratio of the primer DNA.

Second, if, according to the Watson-Crick model, a T-base is laid down complementary to each A-base in the parent DNA, then the frequency with which A is a neighbor to A must be matched by the frequency with which T is a neighbor to T. This was exactly as found (Table V): the sequence ApA (A neighboring A, held together by phosphate) had the same frequency of occurrence as TpT (I, Table V), and CpC the same as GpG (VI, Table V). In the same way, by laying down bases along the parent sequence CpA (II), these would be predicted to be TpG (II) (this is because the strands are laid down in opposite polarity to the parent, see Fig. 7). So the frequency with which radioactive phosphate appeared in Tp after incubation with Gp must be the same as the frequency with which it appeared in Cp after incubation with Ap (II). The same was true for TpC and GpA (III), ApG and CpT (IV), and Apc and GpT (V).

If DNA was made enzymatically with P^{32}-labeled nucleotides (using a very small amount, 5%, of native DNA as primer), the bases in this new DNA had a certain characteristic nearest neighbor frequency: in DNA from calf, for instance, the frequency of C neighboring G was expressed as 0.016. This synthetic calf DNA was now used as a primer, and it was found that the new DNA had exactly the same frequency of C neighboring G, 0.016. If bacterial DNA was made, C neighbored G with quite different frequency (0.050). As Kornberg (1961) says, "Available physical methods do not enable us to distinguish between

TABLE V

NEAREST NEIGHBOR FREQUENCIES OF *Mycobacterium phlei* DNA[a,b]

Reaction no.	Labeled triphosphate	Isolated 3'-deoxyribonucleotide			
		Tp	Ap	Cp	Gp
1	dATP[32]	*a* TpA 0.012	*b* ApA 0.024 I	*c* CpA 0.063 II	*d* GpA 0.065 III
2	dTTP[32]	*b* TpT 0.026 I	*a* ApT 0.031	*d* CpT 0.045 IV	GpT 0.060 V
3	dGTP[32]	*e* TpG 0.063 II	*f* ApG 0.045 IV	*g* CpG 0.139	*h* GpG 0.090 VI
4	dCTP[32]	*f* TpC 0.061 III	*e* ApC 0.064 V	*h* CpC 0.090 VI	*g* GpC 0.122
	Sums	0.162	0.164	0.337	0.337

[a] From Kornberg (1961).

[b] Identical Roman numerals designate those sequence frequencies that should be equivalent in a Watson and Crick DNA model with strands of opposite polarity; identical lower-case letters designate sequence frequencies that should be equivalent in a model with strands of similar polarity. The symbol TpA stands for deoxyadenylyl-(5'-3') deoxythymidine.

Chemical analysis of the base composition of the primer DNA indicated molar proportions of thymine, adenine, cytosine, and guanine of 0.165, 0.162, 0.335, and 0.338, respectively.

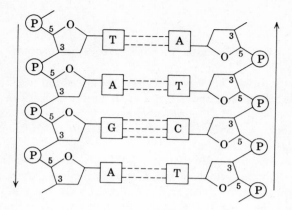

Opposite polarity

TpA (0.012) = TpA (0.012)
ApG (0.045) = CpT (0.045)
GpA (0.065) = TpC (0.061)

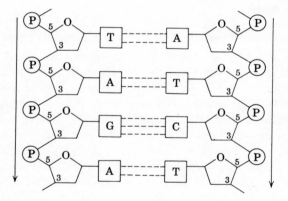

Similar polarity

TpA (0.012) = ApT (0.031)
ApG (0.045) = TpC (0.061)
GpA (0.065) = CpT (0.045)

FIG. 7. Contrast between a Watson and Crick DNA model with strands of opposite polarity and a model with strands of similar polarity. The predicted matching nearest-neighbor sequence frequencies are different. Values in parentheses are sequence frequencies from the experiment with *M. phlei* DNA. [From A. Kornberg, "Enzymatic Syntheses of DNA," p. 24. Wiley, New York, 1961.]

DNA samples of identical base composition as, for example, those isolated from a man and a mouse, or those from a cow and *B. subtilis*. However, by nearest-neighbor frequency analysis, calf thymus DNA can be distinguished from *B. subtilis* DNA."

The enzymatically synthesized DNA, therefore, satisfies these two conditions: it has base complementarity with the known natural DNA, and it reflects in its base sequence the sequence of the primer. One can say, therefore, that Kornberg's enzymatic system in the test tube faithfully does what the enzymes do in the cell during cell division and replication of DNA. It is difficult to overemphasize the importance of this finding. It means that the biologist can now synthesize at will the genetic material of any living thing.

Section III. Rates of Reactions in Living Organisms

What is a living thing? A set of enzymatically catalyzed reactions, separated from the environment by some boundary, and capable of self-duplication. Self-duplication means that the set of reactions must be the same from generation to generation; and during the life span of one generation, the enzymes can, of course, perform only one set of reactions. Therefore, for a living thing to exist, the conditions inside its boundaries must be constant. But the environment outside is far from constant: the bacterial cell encounters a medium lacking a nutrient; the amoeba floats into water with a high salt concentration; the frog swims into icy water in a cold season; the water dries out in the drinking hole of the lion; the crops fail and the man must starve. To meet these circumstances, every living thing has evolved a way to maintain internal constancy in face of external change. One might suppose, once an organism is born and endowed with a set of enzymes which make it take up some of the environment and convert it into living substance, that these enzymes would be there all its life. This was the view held until the late 1930's, when Schoenheimer (1942) discovered, by means of isotopically labeled compounds, *the dynamic state of body constituents.* It was thought until then that all the substances of the cell are laid down during growth, and replaced only if damaged by "wear and tear"; that what we eat is used merely as "fuel"; that the body was like a superior internal combustion engine. A concession was made for "reserve stores" of protein, carbohydrate, or fat, which were used in times of food scarcity, and replaced in times of plenty. But we now know that every body constituent: ribonucleic acids, enzymes, carbohydrates, fats, and mineral elements, within every tissue, even apparently inert ones like tooth or bone or the lens of the eye, is constantly broken down and replaced throughout life. Why should evolution have arrived at what appears to be a wasteful process? The answer is in the one word: flexibility. The organism will be able better to maintain a constant internal environment, in an ever changing external environment, if it is sufficiently flexible. One can easily see that a rapid increase in the synthesis of one substance can be better achieved if the synthesis machinery is working continuously, if the machine is cranked and well oiled, so to speak. Look at arginase, one of the enzymes that participate in the formation of urea; to keep the internal environment of the animal constant, to take care of an excess of urea, an increase in the protein of the animal's diet instantly results in a larger amount of arginase. The animal could do this by having a certain amount of arginase and adding a little more when the necessity arises to make and metabolize more urea. This would mean having to start the activity of those enzymes that make arginase. But if the animal is in the habit of continuously making arginase and breaking it down, the arginase-synthesizing enzymes are all there and working; it needs only a slight shift in favor of increased synthesis.

This explanation of the evolutionary advantage of turnover must be qualified in one sense: it applies in the main to animals. Microorganisms have achieved flexibility in another way, by developing inducible enzymes that can be made from scratch in instant response to a changed environment.

As was pointed out in the discussion on biological damage caused by radiation (Chap. IV, Sect. I-5), an error that accidentally appears in a protein molecule does not remain there for the lifetime of the organism: in the course of turnover, the faulty molecule is broken down and removed, and a new, correct one is synthesized. Thus turnover also has the function of guarding against the accumulation of faulty molecules, produced by errors made in protein synthesis.

1. THE DYNAMIC STATE OF BODY CONSTITUENTS

In the early experiments, Schoenheimer (1942) gave water labeled with heavy hydrogen (D_2O) to rats, and observed the rate of incorporation of isotope into body fat until all the fat was labeled. Later, Shemin and Rittenberg gave a single dose of an amino acid labeled with the heavy nitrogen isotope (N^{15}), which was rapidly incorporated into body proteins. They then studied the gradual disappearance of the heavy nitrogen from various protein fractions (due, of course, to replacement of them by the normal amino acids from the diet). Thus, half the liver protein nitrogen was replaced in 7 days (half-life of liver nitrogen).

It should perhaps be remarked here that though all body constituents are turned over (with the exception of collagen, a connective tissue protein which seems to be completely stable once it is made), their rate of turnover falls into two classes: those organs and substances with a long half-life and those with a short half-life. This discovery was made (Thompson and Ballou, 1956) by giving radioactive (tritium-labeled) water, T_2O, to rats over a period of 125 days. Up to 30% of the hydrogen atoms in body constituents became labeled. The animals were then transferred to ordinary water, and the rate of disappearance (by replacement and resynthesis) of radioactivity in the various tissues was observed. By using tritium, the sensitivity of the method was high enough so that, after rapid elimination of the label from the short-lived components, enough radioactivity remained in the long-lived ones to be easily detectable. It was found that, whereas most of the liver substances had half-lives of 4.5 and of 12 days, one constituent (3%) had a half-life of 140 days. As much as 40% of muscle and 54% of brain had half-lives of 100 and 150 days, respectively. These are very slow turnover rates, if one considers the brief life span of a rat (about 2 years). The impression one gains is that metabolically active components of tissues (e.g., enzymes) turn over rapidly and that structural components do so much more slowly. It has since been shown that even the same substance can, in different tissues, have different rates of turnover.

These experiments told us only about "components" of tissues, or generalized constituents such as "protein nitrogen." With the availability in radioactive form of individual metabolic intermediates, it became possible to study turnover of these compounds.

2. HEMOGLOBIN TURNOVER

An entirely unique case is that of the hemoglobin of the mammalian red blood cells. Its prosthetic group is hemin, the biosynthesis of which has been discussed (Chap. VI, Sect. II-3). Shemin and Rittenberg (1946) studied the incorporation of N^{15}-labeled glycine into hemin in man. On the basis of what we know about turnover of body constituents, one would expect that labeled glycine, after it enters the blood circulation, would gradually be taken up into the red blood cells as more and more of existing hemoglobin is broken down and resynthesized with the participation of the labeled glycine. This process would be expected to reach a maximum when the N^{15}-glycine is used up; then the isotope content of the hemoglobin would decline as unlabeled glycine enters the circulation, and one after another of the hemoglobin molecules, randomly and irrespectively of when they were made, would be destroyed and replaced.

In actual fact, the experimental results turned out to be quite different. After the feeding of labeled glycine stopped, the incorporation into hemoglobin did not decline, but continued for almost 25 days. The label was then not removed gradually, but remained constant for 100 days. Then the isotope content abruptly declined (Fig. 8). The

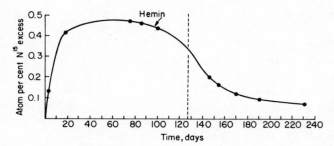

FIG. 8. N^{15} concentration in hemin in man after feeding N^{15}-labeled glycine for 3 days. [From D. Shemin and D. Rittenberg, *J. Biol. Chem.* **166**, 627 (1946).]

conclusions were most surprising: the hemoglobin, and presumably the whole red blood cells, have a definite life span, about 130 days in man. They are not continuously built up and broken down, like other tissues. Given the labeled precursor, a certain batch of red blood cells is synthesized, using the isotopic precursor. This batch lives for 130 days, then is broken down again. The enzymes causing the breakdown do not operate at random, but can recognize cells 130 days old. The destruction is not indiscriminate, but a function of age.

3. TURNOVER; THEORETICAL CONSIDERATIONS

Connected to the concept of turnover, there is, of course, the idea of precursor and product. Anything that is broken down and resynthesized must have a precursor (from which it is synthesized), and a product (into which it is changed). It became possible, with tracers, to explore the rates of metabolic reactions and their kinetics in the bodies of whole, living animals under physiological conditions. Mathematical descriptions were derived of the rates of these reactions and thereby some insight was gained into their quantitative importance.

As put by Zilversmit, the pioneer of these studies, "When one considers the complexity of the animal organism, the multitude of reactions occurring simultaneously, the chemical dissociations and recombinations, the syntheses and destructions incessantly taking place, the shifting of metabolites from one tissue to another, one must marvel at the mechanism whereby the body fluids and tissues maintain their constant chemical compositions. This very constancy precludes the study of the dynamic state by simple chemical determinations of tissue constituents. A new approach to this problem became available with the use of labeling agents, particularly radioactive isotopes, since they could be prepared in negligible, even chemically undetectable quantities associated with large amounts of radiation."

4. DEFINITIONS

First, a few definitions. Implicit in the idea of the dynamic state of body constituents is the concept of the *metabolic pool*. It is the mixture of chemical compounds, circulating in the body (*body pool*) or tissue under consideration (*tissue pool*), which is derived from the diet or from the breakdown of tissue constituents, and which is transformed into other tissue constituents. This pool is in a constant state of flux, with molecules entering and others simultaneously leaving it. Yet the number of molecules present remains the same.

The metabolic pool is subdivided: it can be the pool of a group of substances (e.g., the amino acid pool), or one particular compound (e.g., the glucose pool). Again, this can be compartmentalized into the plasma glucose pool, the liver glucose pool, etc., measuring the amount of glucose present in each of these tissues.

As was hinted above, the pool size in an adult (nongrowing) animal is constant. This means it does not increase or decrease in size, though it is constantly replaced. It is said to be in the *steady state*. *Turnover*, then, means the renewal, by resynthesis or transport into the pool to maintain it in a steady state, of the same number of molecules lost from it by breakdown, transformation, or transport from it. *Turnover rate* signifies the amount of substance turning over per unit time, *turnover time* the time required for turnover of a quantity of substance equal to that present in the pool, and *half-life* the time taken for replacement of substance equal to one half the pool.

As was indicated above, turnover can refer to *chemical* breakdown and resynthesis of the pool, as well as to *transport* in and out of the pool. The one type of turnover concerns the biochemist: he wants to know how much of the pool is chemically replaced per unit time. The physiologist, on the other hand, is interested in turnover of "compartments": the turnover of glucose in the blood compartment, determined by measuring the rate at which glucose enters and leaves the circulation from other tissues. Or the rate of turnover of liver glucose in terms, not of its formation and breakdown, but only of transport into and out of the liver. This leads to some difficulties, because frequently the substance under investigation exchanges rapidly with another substance. Glucose and glycogen are in extremely rapid equilibrium with each other. If one determines the liver glucose pool by isotope experiment, it will appear to be much larger than the free glucose of liver. Therefore, the compartment containing liver glucose presumably also includes glycogen. On the other hand, the "body" pool of free glycine was found to correspond only to the glycine of liver and kidney, not of the whole body, because the method used measured only the glycine rapidly equilibrating with administered glycine in organs such as liver and kidney, and not the slowly equilibrated glycine of muscle. This is probably due to permeability barriers.

The experimental method of making a determination of pool size and turnover is none other than the isotope dilution technique (Chap. V, Sect. I-8), adapted to the whole animal. Again, all the information is derived from specific activities, in this case the rate of change of specific activities.

5. Turnover Experiments; Examples

Take the simplest case (Zilversmit *et al.*, 1943): to measure the turnover rate of blood glucose. A small dose of labeled glucose (B^*) is injected (Fig. 9). It mixes instantly with the unlabeled glucose (B) present in the circulation, which causes the radioactivity of B^* to be diluted, lowering its specific activity. With time, the specific activity of the labeled glucose is further lowered by nonradioactive glucose entering the circulation (no glucose is synthesized in the circulatory system). Of course, glucose also leaves the circulation, by oxidative breakdown, as well as by simple transport out of the blood vessels. But since there is no discrimination between labeled and unlabeled glucose in these processes, the specific activity will not be affected by the glucose *leaving,* only by that *entering* the circulation, as the latter is nonradioactive. Since there is a steady state, and the total glucose remains constant, the turnover of blood glucose can therefore be calculated from the rate of decrease in specific activity of the injected labeled glucose. The only determinations that need be made are of the specific activity of glucose on small samples of blood at different times after one injection of labeled glucose of known specific activity. The rate of change of specific activity, dS_B/dt, depends on the fraction of the

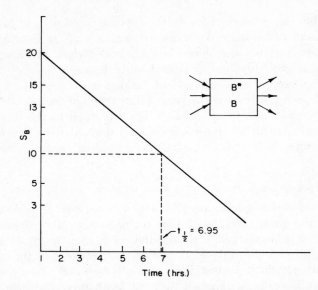

FIG. 9. *Upper right:* Blood constituent B is labeled with a single dose of B^*. New B is delivered to the blood from 3 sources and disappears from the blood by 3 paths. The graph shows the decrease in specific activity (S_B) of B plotted semilogarithmically against time. The half-time $(t_{1/2})$ is the time in which the specific activity of B is halved (for example from 20 to 10) and is here equal to 6.95 hours. [From D. B. Zilversmit *et al.,* 1943.]

blood glucose pool that at time t is radioactive, B^*/B, on the rate of turnover, q, and inversely on the size of the blood glucose pool, B.

Therefore

$$\frac{dS_B}{dt} = -q \frac{B^*}{B} \frac{1}{B}$$

where S_B is the specific activity of the glucose. Since

$$\frac{B^*}{B} = S_B$$

therefore

$$\frac{dS_B}{dt} = -q \frac{S_B}{B}$$

But in a steady state q and B are constant, therefore

$$\frac{dS_B}{dt} = -kS_B$$

Integrating, one obtains

$$S_B = S_B{}^0 e^{-kt}$$

where $S_B{}^0$ is the specific activity of B at zero time (time of injection), and e the base of the natural logarithm. This is the equation for an exponential decay curve. Therefore, upon plotting the log of S_B against time, one obtains a straight line which can be extrapolated to zero time to give $S_B{}^0$, the specific activity of glucose at zero time. This will, of course, be less than that of the injected glucose, by a factor a. The weight of labeled glucose injected, when multiplied by the dilution factor a, gives the weight of the body pool of glucose. The time it takes for one half of this to disappear (or for the specific activity to reach one half) is the half-life ($t_{1/2}$) of glucose, which can be read off the graph, or calculated from the slope (i.e., k):

$$\frac{1}{k} = \frac{t_{1/2}}{\ln 2} = \frac{t_{1/2}}{0.693}$$

Also, k being the turnover rate, $1/k$ is the turnover time.

Thus body pool, half-life, turnover rate, and turnover time can be calculated from a set of specific activity–time points.

These determinations can be made easily by specific activity determinations on blood samples, as for instance in a comparison of the turnover of glucose on fasting and on feeding (Russell, 1957). Sometimes it is enough to determine specific activities of the compound excreted in urine.

If it has only a brief and fleeting existence, one can trap it; for instance, by injecting a foreign amine, together with labeled acetate. The amine will be acetylated by body acetate (and pyruvate), and excreted in the urine. In this way, the acetate (plus pyruvate) pool and its turnover (15–20 mmoles per day per 100 gm. body weight) have been estimated, though acetate and pyruvate themselves are not normally excreted. To get at protein pools, one might have to resort to biopsies or start with a number of animals, one or several of which are killed at different times after injection for specific activity determinations.

One important assumption is made in all the above calculations: the injected labeled compound is diluted only by unlabeled compound; no labeled substance returns after it has left the pool. Special equations have been derived for cases where label returns to the pool, such as the transfer of potassium ions between plasma and red blood cells. Here, an *equilibrium* specific activity is reached and the straight-line plot is made of the log of plasma specific activity minus equilibrium specific activity against time. The half-time of the exchange was found to be 121 minutes.

When plotting log of specific activity against time, composite curves are sometimes obtained with different slopes, indicating a removal of the compound or ion at different rates. For instance, sodium ions from plasma appear to be transferred across capillary walls at different rates in different areas of the circulation.

6. Turnover Experiments by Continuous Infusion

A method of administering the isotopic compound, more satisfactory than the single-injection method but more difficult to carry out in practice, is the constant infusion technique (continuous injection at a known rate). This maintains constant specific activity of the administered compound within the organism. Whereas, for the single injection technique, *two* log of specific activity points must be plotted against time to determine the slope (in practice, for a satisfactory curve, many more are of course needed), the constant infusion technique needs only *one* point. This is a consequence of the fact that turnover determination is merely a variant of the isotope dilution method, so that the fundamental isotope dilution equation (Chap. V, Sect. I-8) holds here also: *total* radioactivity of the injected material (B^*) must be the same before dilution with the unlabeled material (B) generated by the animal, as after dilution:

$$S_B R = S_b(r + R)$$

Hence

$$r = R\left(\frac{S_B}{S_b} - 1\right)$$

where S_B is the specific activity of the infused labeled compound, S_b the new specific activity of the compound after dilution in the body, R the rate of infusion (in terms of weight), and r the rate of synthesis by the organism of the compound. Since, in the steady state, rate of synthesis equals rate of breakdown, r is then the turnover rate. This can be calculated simply by dividing the infusion rate R^* (in terms of radioactivity, counts per minute per minute) by the specific activity of the compound in the body, S_b.

For instance, Sabine and Johnson (1964) used this method to determine the production of acetate by a ruminant: a lightly anesthetized sheep was given labeled acetate of known specific activity (S_B) by continuous injection at a known rate (R^*) through the jugular vein into the bloodstream. Small blood samples were withdrawn periodically for specific activity determinations of acetate. Equilibrium was reached after 30 minutes of continuous infusion: specific activity of blood acetate (S_b) was then constant. From it, the investigators calculated a turnover rate of 5.2 millimoles per hour per kg. body weight. Infusion was then stopped, and the log of decrease in specific activity was plotted against time. This plot gave a half-life of acetate of 1.0–1.5 minutes. The body pool determined therefrom was 6.2 millimoles. The pool size of acetate divided by the concentration of acetate (millimoles per liter) gave the value in liters of the animal's body occupied by the acetate. If converted to per cent of the known body volume of the sheep, this "acetate space" was calculated to be 20%.

For an experiment such as this to give figures that approximate true values, the following conditions must be fulfilled: the infused isotopic compound mixes instantaneously with the body pool; the animal is truly in a steady state; the "space" occupied by the compound and its concentration are constant throughout the experiment; and, most important, no labeled acetate returns to the pool. This last condition is certainly not fulfilled in the above experiment. But separate tests revealed that the returned labeled acetate was negligibly small.

Instead of continuous infusion, which requires continuous intravenous injection, it is possible to achieve the same objective by feeding the isotopic compound over long periods of time. Amino acid synthesis was studied in this way with feeding of labeled glycine for 39 days by Arnstein and Neuberger. The rate of glycine synthesis by the rat was determined to be 2.5 millimoles per day per 100 gm. body weight.

An elaborate and highly informative experiment on the same principle provided information on the cholesterol pool and turnover rate in man, with feeding of tritium-labeled cholesterol to patients over a prolonged period (LeRoy *et al.*, 1957). The pool size was found to be 61 gm., the turnover rate 8.8 gm. per day.

7. Precursor-Product Relationships

The idea of turnover implies that for every substance broken down and resynthesized there must be another compound, the parent of the substance turned over, from which it is made. This compound is called the "precursor"; it is changed into the "product." Specific activity measurements on pairs of substances, suspected to be precursor and product, can reveal whether they are indeed related to each other in this way. Further, mathematical interpretation of the relationship can reveal facts about the equilibrium state between them in the living animal. It should be noted that "precursor" can be either the compound which undergoes *chemical* transformation, or that which is *transported* from one tissue to another. For instance, acetate is a precursor of cholesterol; and liver cholesterol is a precursor of plasma cholesterol.

Let us consider an ideal situation, in which a radioactive compound A is injected into the bloodstream of an animal. In the liver, A is transformed into B. Specific activity measurements of liver A (precursor) and liver B (product) are made at definite times after injection. When curves are plotted of these values against time, their shapes are as illustrated in Fig. 10. A mathematical derivation for the curves is given by Zilversmit *et al.* (1943). However, one can see intuitively that the specific activity curve for A would at first rise, as more and more of the nonradioactive A of the liver becomes mixed with radioactive A entering from the blood, until the supply of radioactive A from the blood is exhausted. At that moment, the specific activity of liver A reaches its maximum. All this time, radioactive as well as nonradioactive A is also *removed* from the liver, since it is being changed into B. Therefore, new radioactive B (derived from A) is added to existing B and *its* specific activity rises, though it is lower than that of A. This is because the radioactive A, after conversion to radioactive B, is further diluted by nonradioactive B. We assume a steady state (constant concentrations of A and B). Therefore, the specific activity of A declines again after it has reached its maximum point, since it is now being diluted with nonradioactive A produced from other sources to replenish the A lost by conversion to B. The specific activity of B, of course, continues to rise during that period. At the moment at which the specific activity of A *equals* that of B (where the curves intersect), B has reached its maximum specific activity and it then declines. It is clear to see that the decline in the specific activity of A is caused

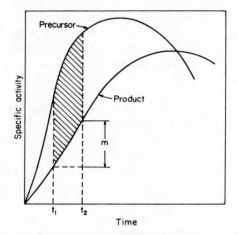

FIG. 10. Specific activity-time relations between product and precursor. [From D. B. Zilversmit *et al.*, *J. Gen. Physiol.* **26**, 325–331 (1943).]

by its conversion to B. The specific activity of B, therefore, rises until it is the same as that of A. It cannot rise higher than this point (intersection point), as obviously the specific activity of the product cannot be higher than that of the precursor *and* continue to rise. From that point on the curve for B also must decline. In other words, the curves intersect at the maximum of B.

The following, then, can be said of any pair of compounds: if the specific activity–time curve of one intersects the second at its peak, the first is the immediate precursor of the second. This has proved to be a fruitful relationship in the identification of precursors. It must, of course, be an *immediate* precursor; that is, no large pools of other intermediates must intervene between precursor and product, themselves liable to turnover at various rates. However, if the immediate precursor is not known, or cannot be isolated, a more distant precursor can be used for the determination, provided its specific activity is close to that of the immediate precursor.

One example will illustrate the power of the method (Spiro, 1959). Glucosamine (Fig. 11) is a sugar derivative

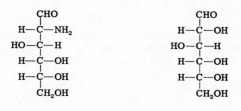

FIG. 11. Glucosamine.   FIG. 12. Glucose.

which occurs in relatively high concentration in blood serum, bound to protein. The questions were: is it synthesized directly from blood glucose (Fig. 12), and is the liver the site of its synthesis? C^{14}-glucose was injected into a number of rats. Blood samples were taken and analyzed for quantity and radioactivity of glucose and glucosamine (i.e., specific activity). Some of the animals were killed after different time intervals, from 45 minutes to 48 hours after injection, and liver glucosamine was determined. The graphs in Fig. 13 show that the specific activity curve of liver glucosamine intersects that of serum glucosamine at the maximum of the latter. Hence, liver glucosamine is the direct precursor of blood glucosamine. Therefore, the liver is the site of glucosamine synthesis. However, as can be seen in Fig. 13, the serum glucose curve does not fit into

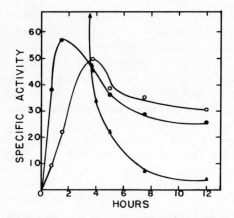

Fig. 13. The relationship of the specific activities of the serum glucose (▲), liver glucosamine (●), and serum glucosamine (○) after the injection of C^{14}-glucose. The mean specific activities for each time are plotted as c.p.m. per μmole of glucose or glucosamine. All values are adjusted to 5.0×10^6 c.p.m. injected into a 250-gm. rat. [From R. G. Spiro, *J. Biol. Chem.* **234**, 742 (1959).]

this picture. The author suggested that the following scheme could account for this anomaly:

$$\text{Serum glucose} \rightarrow \text{liver glucosamine} \rightleftharpoons \text{serum glucosamine} \rightarrow Y$$
$$\downarrow$$
$$X$$

(X and Y are other unknown metabolites)

Here, glucosamine *returns* to the liver; in fact, liver and serum glucosamine can be considered as part of a common pool. If the specific activity for glucosamine is recalculated for a common liver and serum pool and plotted against time, a new relationship (Fig. 14) is found, which shows that serum glucose is in fact the immediate precursor of the joint liver-serum glucosamine.

In addition to this information, it is possible to obtain turnover rate and time from these curves as well as, if not better than, from the log of specific activity–time curves already mentioned (Chap. VI, Sect. II-5).

As discussed at some length (Chap. VI, Sect. II-13), the coding of amino acids in protein synthesis is mediated through RNA, which carries the code from DNA to protein. The DNA occurs only in the cell nucleus, protein synthesis mostly in the cytoplasm. Therefore, the RNA must be made in the nucleus and migrate to the cytoplasm.

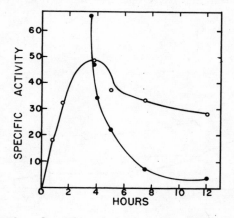

Fig. 14. The relationship of the specific activities of the serum glucose (●) and the glucosamine of the liver and serum considered as a common pool (○). Values are expressed as in Fig. 13. [From R. G. Spiro, *J. Biol. Chem.* **234**, 742 (1959).]

This is borne out in experiments: when labeled uridine, a precursor of RNA, is given an animal, autoradiography shows that radioactivity is incorporated first in the nuclear RNA and only later in the cytoplasmic RNA. But where in the nucleus is RNA made? In the chromatin, or the nucleolus, or both? Or is it made in the chromatin and then passes through the nucleolus into the cytoplasm? Amano and Leblond (1960) give an answer to these questions. They injected a labeled RNA precursor (tritium-labeled cytidine) into mice, then made autoradiographs of liver cells at different times after injection. The quantity of RNA in the nucleus was measured by its color intensity determined by a microspectrophotometer, after a specific staining procedure. The radioactivity was assayed by exposure to X-ray film, and counting of silver grains blackened in the emulsion of the film. This gave the specific activities of RNA. The specific activity–time curves are shown in Fig. 15. The chromatin RNA curve is independent of the two

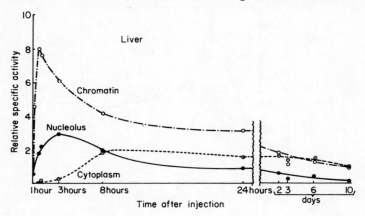

FIG. 15. Time curves of the relative specific activity of RNA calculated as a ratio of the number of silver grains per unit area over the relative RNA concentration. Mean relative RNA concentrations in chromatin, nucleolus, and cytoplasm were respectively 1.0, 7.3, and 4.1 in liver parenchymal cells. [From M. Amano and C. P. Leblond, *Exptl. Cell Res.* **20**, 250 (1960).]

others. The nucleolus RNA curve intersects the cytoplasmic RNA curve at the latter's maximum. It is therefore clear that RNA is synthesized both in chromatin and in the nucleolus. The chromatin RNA breaks down again, whereas the RNA synthesized in the nucleolus migrates to the cytoplasm, presumably taking there its message for protein synthesis. A plain clear-cut answer to a plain clear-cut question—a model of how a scientific experiment should be conducted.

It happens rarely, in metabolic reactions, that there is complete transfer of a compound from one place to another, or complete transformation from one form to another. There are usually several intermediates, each having a pool of its own which may be fed from other sources and may feed into other sources than those of the transfer under consideration. If a transfer is reversible, the complexity increases still further, since a product may at the same time behave like a precursor.

Nonetheless, differential equations have been set up to express the rates of transport, transformation, or excretion, the size of pools involved, and, generally, the kinetics of reactions in living organisms. These have been reviewed extensively (Russell, 1957). For instance, if in the sequence

$$\text{Protein} \overset{1}{\rightleftharpoons} \text{amino acid pool} \rightarrow \text{urea in body fluids} \rightarrow \text{urea excreted}$$
$$\uparrow$$
$$\text{Food}$$

isotopic amino acid (e.g., N^{15}-glycine) is introduced, the disappearance of the isotope from the various compartments (protein, amino acid pool, the two urea pools) can be described by a set of differential equations, involving the rates of reaction in the directions indicated by the arrows. These can be integrated and with certain observations (rate of food intake, rate of urea excretion, maximum excretion of isotope in urea), the rates of reactions 1 and 2 can be calculated.

8. ALTERNATIVE METABOLIC PATHWAYS

It is obvious from these considerations that alternative metabolic pathways exist for almost all metabolites. For example, amino acids can be derived from breakdown of protein or from uptake of food. Glucose is the precursor of glycogen, galactose, glucosamine, and glucuronic acid. The particular pathway taken by a molecule of glucose at a given moment depends on a multiplicity of factors, often hormonal, which can be studied properly only in the intact animal under the normal control and regulation of metabolism. Therefore, a quantitative study of metabolic pathways and sequences is not possible with isolated tissues, and requires the use of isotopic compounds in the whole animal.

From the vast literature on alternative metabolic pathways, such as, for instance, the metabolism of glucose through the Embden-Meyerhoff and the pentose phosphate pathways (Katz and Wood, 1960), only one example can be given here. This is the work of Freedman and Graff (1958): pyruvate is known to be the branchpoint of a number of metabolic pathways. Two of these are the alternative ways for pyruvate to enter the Krebs cycle (Fig. 2). It can (a) lose CO_2 by decarboxylation to give acetate which combines with oxalacetate to form citrate, a member of the Krebs cycle; or it can (b) combine with CO_2 to form oxalacetate, another member of the cycle. In case (a), there is no net increase in the amount of cycle intermediates, and the pyruvate is used for energy purposes only. In case (b), the amount of cycle intermediates increases by one molecule for each molecule of pyruvate which enters. This new oxalacetate can then be used for synthetic purposes, as for instance by amination to aspartic acid as a building block for new protein.

The authors wanted to find out how the feeding or fasting of rats would determine which pathway is taken by pyruvate. The distribution of label in one member of the Krebs cycle, ketoglutaric acid (KG), indicates the way labeled pyruvate enters the cycle (Fig. 2). Put the label into position 2 of pyruvate. Then, if pathway (a) is followed, much of the activity must appear in carbon 5 of KG (cf. Table III). If pathway (b) is taken, carbons 2 and 3 of KG would be labeled. In the actual experiment, alanine-2-C^{14} was injected instead of pyruvate, and glutamic acid isolated in place of KG, since both these amino acids are in rapid equilibrium with their respective keto acids (see Fig. 2). Freedman and Graff discovered that in the fasted rat, upon injection of alanine-2-C^{14} which gives rise to pyruvate-2-C^{14}, over 80% of the radioactivity of the glutamic acid was in carbons 2 and 3. In the fed rats, the most highly labeled carbon atom was in position 5. Therefore, in the fasted rat pathway (*b*), and in the fed rat pathway (*a*), is operative. A metabolic control mechanism must therefore exist, which directs the respective enzymes to increase and decrease according to the demands of the situation, by change either in quantity or in activity. This change then brings about the switch from one to the other pathway. It makes sense in respect to the economy of the starving organism to increase the amount of Krebs cycle intermediates from pyruvate (and therefore ultimately from carbohydrate), since these intermediates can be used for amino acid and protein synthesis. The fed rat has no need to manufacture amino acids; it can therefore afford to burn the pyruvate directly through decarboxylation and reactions of the Krebs cycle.

REFERENCES

Amano, N., and Leblond, C. P. (1960). *Exptl. Cell Res.* **20**, 250.

Bassham, J. H. (1962). *Sci. American* **206**, 88.

Brenner, S., Jacob, F., and Meselson, M. (1961). *Nature* **190**, 576.

Calvin, M., and Bassham, J. A. (1957). "The Path of Carbon in Photosynthesis." Prentice-Hall, Englewood Cliffs, New Jersey.

Dintzis, H. M. (1961). *Proc. Natl. Acad. Sci. U. S.* **47**, 247.

Freedman, A. D., and Graff, S. (1958). *J. Biol. Chem.* **233**, 292.

Giacomoni, D., and Spiegelman, S. (1962). *Science* **138**, 1328.

Hall, B. D., and Spiegelman, S. (1961). *Proc. Natl. Acad. Sci. U. S.* **47**, 137 and 1135.

Katz, J., and Wood, H. G. (1960). *J. Biol. Chem.* **235**, 2165.

Kornberg, A. (1961). "Enzymatic Synthesis of DNA." Wiley, New York.

Lane, M. D., Halenz, D. R., Kosow, D. B., and Hegre, C. S. (1960). *J. Biol. Chem.* **235**, 3082.

Langdon, R. G., and Bloch, K. (1953). *J. Biol. Chem.* **200**, 129 and 135.

LeRoy, G. V., Gould, R. G., Bergenstal, D. M., Werbin, H., and Kabara, J. J. (1957). *J. Lab. Clin. Med.* **49**, 858.

Levinthal, C., Keynan, A., and Higa, A. (1962). *Proc. Natl. Acad. Sci. U. S.* **48**, 1631.

Little, H. N., and Bloch, K. (1950). *J. Biol. Chem.* **183**, 33.

Meselson, M., and Stahl, F. W. (1958). *Proc. Nat. Acad. Sci. U. S.* **44**, 671.

Peterkofsky, A. (1962). *J. Biol. Chem.* **237**, 787.

Rich, A. (1962). *In* "Horizons in Biochemistry" (M. Kasha, ed.), p. 103. Academic Press, New York.

Russell, J. A. (1957). *Perspectives in Biol. Med.* **1**, 138.

Sabine, J. R., and Johnson, B. C. (1964). *J. Biol. Chem.* **239**, 89.

Schoenheimer, R. (1942). "The Dynamic State of Body Constituents." Harvard Univ. Press, Cambridge.

Shemin, D., and Kumin, S. (1952). *J. Biol. Chem.* **198**, 827.

Shemin, D., and Rittenberg, D. (1946). *J. Biol. Chem.* **166**, 627.

Shemin, D., and Wittenberg, J. (1951). *J. Biol. Chem.* **192**, 315.

Spiro, R. G. (1959). *J. Biol. Chem.* **234**, 742.

Thompson, R. C., and Ballou, J. E. (1956). *J. Biol. Chem.* **223**, 795.

von Ehrenstein, H., and Lipmann, F. (1961). *Proc. Natl. Acad. Sci. U. S.* **47**, 941.

Wüersch, J., Huang, R. L., and Bloch, K. (1952). *J. Biol. Chem.* **195**, 439.

Zamecnik, P. C. (1960). *Harvey Lectures* **54**, 256.

Zilversmit, D. B., Entenman, C., and Fishler, M. C. (1943). *J. Gen. Physiol.* **26**, 325 and 333.

INDEX